FACTS ABOUT

FIN-
LAND

FACTS ABOUT

FIN-
LAND

OTAVA PUBLISHING COMPANY LTD.
HELSINKI

Principal articles witten by:
PÄIVI ELOVAINIO, Dr.Pol.Sc., Senior lecturer
MAX JAKOBSON, Minister
HANNA OJANEN, Dr.Pol.Sc.
JUKKA TARKKA, Dr.Pol.Sc.
ALLAN TIITTA, Ph.D., Senior lecturer
KAIJA VALKONEN, M.A.
JYRKI VESIKANSA, Lic. Pol
OSMO A. WIIO, Dr. Soc. Sc.
SEPPO ZETTERBERG, Ph. D., Professor

Updated information
in internet:
http://virtual.finland.fi

English translation: Timothy Binham
Graphic design: Katja Alanen
Layout: Kari Koski
Cover design: Maija Vallinoja

Printed by:
Otava Book Printing Co.
Keuruu 1999

ISBN 951-1-15514-8

Contents

Finland
in Europe

Naturally Finland did not become a part of Europe by joining the European Union. Finland has always been European, the northernmost country of the subcontinent. And yet membership meant a crucial change in the relationship between Finland and Europe. It seems to have brought the two closer together, even geographically, as it were. Of course Finland is located at a considerable distance from most of Europe. Despite being in the EU, Finland is left off the weather map in many major European newspapers. Nonetheless, Finland is no longer the exotic extremity of the inhabited world, *Finis terra*, to which only the bravest explorers dared venture, but increasingly a country that is present in many ways as a part of Europe. If during the membership negotiations Finland still seemed remote and unfathomably northern from the EU perspective it is now becoming increasingly familiar and comprehensible. People are accustomed to seeing Finland at the negotiating table, discussing common goals and problems, and its distinctive features and concerns are beginning to be known.

Meanwhile, the Finns have become more familiar with Europe through EU membership. This goes particularly for the union itself and how it functions, but also for the other Member States, whose views and

◀ Although in 1889 Finland was still a grand duchy of the Russian Empire, it had its own pavilion at the Paris World Fair. Here, Mme Paris receiving the young damsel Finland, who bears a representation of Helsinki Cathedral on her hat. A further symbolic note is added by the parcels in the boat, marked E.U. (*Exposition Universelle*).

The Member States of the European Union (green) and the countries with which negotiations preparing accession began in 1999.

objectives the Finns are now following and taking into account more than ever before.

The Finnish debate on joining the Union focused on the twin concepts of solidarity with the West and Finland's distinctive character. There was much talk of "entering Europe", and comparisons were made between things Finnish and European. To Finnish eyes, 'European' means something slightly better than 'Finnish', a worldly-wise suavity beyond the reach of the clumsy Finns. Without a doubt, the Finns have a special attitude, curiosity mixed with admiration, towards foreign countries and Europe in particular. Finland has also been perceived as an innovative country excited by novelty, where the latest technological inventions promptly become part of everyday life, as Angel Ganivet, Spanish consul in Helsinki, observed one hundred years ago. In those days,

■ The euro coins to be introduced into circulation in 2002 will have national symbols on one side. The coin to be released in Finland will depict a swan, representing Finnish nature, and the cent a lion, from the country's coat of arms.

telephones and bicycles were all the rage; today, one Finn in two has a mobile phone.

Perhaps the attraction of things European and the ease with which we adopt innovations have helped Finland quickly understand the essence of the European Union. Within a few years it has been accepted as a Member State to be reckoned with and an implicitly trusted Community partner. Finland has also been praised for its constructive attitude. The Finns are receiving, with some embarrassment, quite flattering compliments; in an interview with a Swedish newspaper, one official of an international organization went so far as to say that any organization would be strengthened by having Finland as its member.

Increasing participation

Finland's relations with Europe and European cooperation were a highly political issue during the Cold War. Integration and economic relations were part of our foreign and security policy, controlled by a policy of neutrality.

Good international relations have always been crucial for a small country like Finland. A favourable international climate extended Finland's freedom of action and opportunities to participate in international affairs. Thus Finland sought to promote détente within the CSCE process and by hosting meetings between the leaders of the superpowers. During the Cold War, in particular, Finland's relations with Western Europe were determined rather on the basis of major political trends than as a result of any independent policy or stance on European integration. At the same time, economic relations with the West were vital. These sometimes took on rather curious forms. Seeking to maintain good relations with both economic blocs, Finnish politics were a balancing act to reconcile an increased say in international affairs with neutrality.

Finland's neutrality excluded any cooperation involving new political obligations or supranational aspects and thus restricting national sovereignty or conflicting with the country's existing obligations. The Agreement on Friendship, Cooperation and Mutual Assistance (usually referred to by its Finnish acronym YYA), concluded between the

◀ Finland hosted the Conference on Security and Cooperation in Europe in 1975. President Urho Kekkonen in discussion with French President Valéry Giscard d'Estaing and British Prime Minister Harold Wilson.

lande   France   Grande-I

► During the Cold War, the Nordic Council was founded by Denmark, Finland, Sweden, Norway and Iceland. The Council sought to increase Nordic cooperation in the sphere of free movement and other fields. The NORDEK free trade area, however, did not get off the ground. The picture shows the Nordic prime ministers churning out proposals.

Soviet Union and Finland in 1948, included a commitment not to join an alliance against the other party or to support such an alliance. It also committed Finland to defending its territory from being used for mounting an attack on the Soviet Union – and, if the international situation so required, to do so in cooperation with the Soviet Union on the basis of consultations.

After the war, Finland cautiously began to re-establish economic relations with the West. The aim of staying outside superpower conflicts of interest hampered participation in various joint projects. Like the Soviet Union, Finland refused Marshall aid, seeking to develop its economic relations with the west by other means, such as joining the International Monetary Fund, the World Bank and GATT. With the Soviet Union, Finland signed a bilateral trade agreement in 1947. International economic cooperation, and membership in organizations promot-

ing such cooperation, was particularly important with respect to Finland's goals of increased trade, industrial competitiveness, economic growth and stability. At the same time, of course, Finland was careful not to concede a competitive edge to its neighbours Sweden and Norway.

The various forms of cooperation developed between the Nordic countries in the 1930s were channelled in the late 1940s into a plan to establish a Nordic customs union. The Soviet Union viewed this project with suspicion. Nordic cooperation was essential to Finland, which stressed the apolitical nature of the planned cooperation and pointed out that it did not cover foreign and security policy. When the Nordic Council was founded in 1952, Finland was not in a position to join immediately, although of course it took a keen interest in the new organization's work. Finland was also prepared to advance further on the road to

The heads of state of Finland and neighbouring countries pay each other frequent visits.

▲ ▲ ▲ Sweden's young king Carl XVI Gustav and President Urho Kekkonen used to hunt together.

▲ ▲ President Boris Yeltsin last visited Finland in 1997. Here, President Martti Ahtisaari greets him and Naina Yeltsina.

▲ President Lennart Meri of Estonia and Martti Ahtisaari waving to a crowd of spectators.

Nordic integration by joining a planned Nordic free trade area. By the late 1950s, however, the other Nordic countries were one step ahead: the launching of negotiations on the European Free Trade Association (EFTA) significantly increased the number of countries to be involved in trade cooperation.

EFTA was initially a pronouncedly Western organization, as it included many members of the North Atlantic Treaty Organization (NATO). The periodic tensions in Soviet-Finnish relations reduced Finland's chances of joining EFTA. As President Kekkonen pointed out in 1961, the Finnish paradox was that the better Finland managed to preserve the Soviet Union's trust as a peaceful neighbour, the better the prospects for cooperation with the West were. Finland managed to attain its objectives by means of special arrangements to reduce the political content of economic cooperation.

With respect to EFTA, this was achieved with the FINEFTA Agreement, concluded with the organization's members in 1961. Under this agreement, Finland was not a member of the organization, although in practice it enjoyed the benefits of membership. Meanwhile, Finland balanced out the influence of EFTA by concluding an agreement with the Soviet Union on lowering customs tariffs. The FINEFTA Agreement took account of Finland's trade relations with the Soviet Union and omitted the reference made in the EFTA Charter to development of relations with the European Economic Community (EEC).

Formally, Finland also stayed outside the Organization for European Economic Cooperation (OEEC), but signed a separate protocol on trade liberalization with its members. In 1968, however, Finland became a member of OEEC's successor, the Organization for Economic Cooperation and Development (OECD).

Finland did not join the Council of Europe until 1989, although it had already participated in the Council's activities for some time by then. It hosted several conferences held by the Council and managed some Council projects.

With regard to Finland's economic goals, membership in some larger economic grouping would have been an advantage. As it was, however, talks on a Nordic economic union (Nordek) foundered in 1969. The plan contained several elements of uncertainty from the point of view of Soviet-Finnish relations, all the more so as some of the prospective participants saw it as no more than a bridge to membership in the European Economic Community.

Since neither the Nordic union nor EEC membership could be reconciled with neutrality, Finland sought and obtained a free trade agreement with the EEC. Negotiations began on Finland's initiative in 1970, and the agreement came into force in 1974. Characteristically for Finland's integration policy, the agreement was accompanied by several measures aimed at safeguarding good neighbourly relations with the Soviet Union. The Finnish agreement with the EEC differed from other Community free trade agreements in that it lacked all references to deepening relations in the future. Finland also concluded a cooperation agreement with the Council of Mutual Economic Assistance (Comecon) and bilateral agreements on removing trade barriers with the socialist countries of Eastern Europe, and developed its trade relations with the Soviet Union along similar lines.

Security policy was a key factor in the formulation of Finland's integration efforts. A credible policy of neutrality was considered to be the best security guarantee. The goal was to maintain Finland's political room for manoeuvre and independent decision-making capacity, while promoting integration that would not bind the country too closely to either side. Gradually Finland established a unique set of symmetrical agreements: unlike any other country, it had, at least in principle, the same kind of trade relations with countries on either side of the Iron Curtain.

From selective to comprehensive participation

When West European integration began to deepen in the mid 1980s, Finland's policy towards integration also entered a new phase. Increasing cooperation between EFTA and the EC had previously been problematical from the Finnish point of view. Gradually, however, EFTA became a key channel of action for Finland. Finland began to view the development of EFTA with increasing favour, seeing that the organization was able to promote its members' interests vis-à-vis the strengthening European Community. Finland finally became a full member of EFTA in 1986 – although this did not change the country's status much in practice, so close the FINEFTA agreement had been to full membership. Reinforcement of EFTA was thought to be a useful way for a neutral country to increase its economic exchanges.

The idea of an extensive European economic zone covering both the EC and EFTA began to take shape in the mid 1980s. For the neutral EFTA countries, this would, as it were, represent a substitute for EC membership without encroaching on their neutrality. In 1989 Jacques Delors, President of the European Commission, made an official proposal on a European Economic Area (EEA), which was to extend the Common Market to the EFTA countries. Thus they could avoid being marginalized by the ever deeper EC integration following upon the Single European Act and the development of the single market. On the other hand, the agreement did not entail unreasonable political obligations for the neutral countries. Meanwhile, the EEA was a good solution for the EC, too: allowing the neutrals to participate in economic cooperation without assuming the economic responsibilities and political goals of European integration obviously would have given rise to objections.

Finland was in favour of general European cooperation, and the EEA was expected to improve its competitiveness and provide an opportunity to take part in making decisions concerning the whole economic area. This was, however, to take place entirely on a free-trade basis: foreign and security policy as well as agricultural policy would not be involved. The unanimity requirement would preserve the participants' national freedom of action and the opportunity to pursue a policy of neutrality.

The structure of the EEA presented problems, however, as the intended equality between EFTA and EC member states was hard to put into practice. It was difficult to permit the participation of EFTA countries in EEA decisions without giving them an unfair advantage in exerting an influence on Community legislation and development while remaining outside it.

Austria applied for EC membership in summer 1989. Even in Finland, the third government report on integration policy, submitted in spring 1990, no longer unequivocally ruled out membership: it was beginning to be considered as an option in the event that the EEA failed to materialize. The report stressed the economic benefits of integration, considering that the EEA would ensure a level playing field for Finland and safeguard the country's economic interests, which were very close to those of the Community. Staying outside would weaken Finland's competitiveness.

The EEA Agreement came into force in 1994, enlarging the internal market of the Community to cover the EFTA countries with the exception of Switzerland. With the agreement, a great deal of Community legislation became applicable in Finland: only trade, agriculture and foreign policy remained outside its scope, along with economic and monetary union (EMU) and cooperation in home affairs introduced with the

Treaty of Maastricht.

Even before the EEA Agreement took effect, most of the EFTA countries applied for EC membership. Austria's application, and even more the application subsequently submitted by Sweden, made Finland view the agreement in a new light. It became increasingly clear that there was a serious gap between the rights and obligations created by it. The EFTA countries realized that they would have little influence on decisions. Only equal participation in decision-making would give them a real say in integration.

The EEA was beginning to look more and more like a temporary solution. In January 1992 the Government therefore proposed submitting an application for membership, estimating that while membership would give the country the chance for a real say in integration, the EEA would only mean unilateral adaptation.

Parliament voted in favour of the proposal – 108 MPs voted for it, 55 against and 32 abstained – and Finland submitted its application on 18 March 1992. Negotiations began in February 1993 and were concluded in March 1994. The result of the referendum held in October that year was 57% for and 43% against membership.

Finland, Austria and Sweden joined the European Union on 1 January 1995. Finland's decision was dictated by both economic and security policy considerations. After Sweden had applied for membership in July 1991, it soon became clear that Finland would have to follow suit in order to avoid conceding a competitive edge to its neighbour. Finland also went through a serious economic crisis in the early '90s. Owing to the collapse of trade with the Soviet Union – in 1992 it only represented 4% of Finland's total foreign trade, as

against a quarter in the early 1980s – and other reasons, including the consequences of the liberalization of capital markets, unemployment soared to a shocking 20%. It was believed that EU membership would help Finland surmount the crisis and give it more control over economic developments.

Another factor that made EU membership look attractive at the time was the uncertainty stemming from the disintegration of the Soviet Union and the instability of Russia. Security arguments in fact played a decisive role in the membership debate. It was thought that joining the EU would indirectly reinforce Finland's security, which the EEA Agreement alone would fail to do.

The many radical changes going on in Europe were naturally also behind the decision. The political map of Europe was being redrawn. The attitude of the Soviet Union towards Finland's economic relations with the West, and towards the European Community itself, had shifted from hostility towards a recognition of the potential benefits of cooperation. The 1988 agreement between the EC and Comecon marked the establishment of official relations and the Soviet Union's recognition of the Community. 1989 saw the signing of an economic framework agreement between the Soviet Union and the EC; also in that year, President Gorbachev stated that Finland was free to decide for itself on its relations with the Community.

Finland had gradually increased its contacts with the EC from 1964, when it first accredited an ambassador to the organization. Finland and the EC Commission initiated a political dialogue in the late 1980s, and Finland invited the Commission to set up a representation in Helsinki.

The Finnish foreign policy doctrine had shifted from neutrality towards nonalignment. The first step on this path was to restrict neutrality to the issues – admittedly many – on which the superpowers differed. The next step was to consider that neutrality was compatible with economic cooperation; this made it possible to start dismantling the cumbersome, symmetrical trade agreements concluded after the war. In 1992, the crucial aspect of neutrality was defined as military nonalignment, remaining outside military alliances in order to remain neutral in the event of war; this was made possible by a credible national defence capability.

Finally, by 1990 the EC itself was beginning to be ready for new enlargement. Following the more immediate accession of the EFTA countries, another enlargement with an even greater long-term impact began to be envisaged, extending the European Union to Central and Eastern Europe.

Finland's membership in the EU reflects the general logic of participation in European affairs: as critical decisions are increasingly made outside the country's own borders, participation in making those decisions becomes more important. The new element, however, is that Finland's participation is no longer based on special arrangements. Whereas the country has previously tended to wait for the dust of change to settle before taking a stand on international developments and integration and trying to mould its international commitments to suit its needs, Finland now engages in a more immediate and, above all, a more unreserved participation. Within the European Union, the Finns have laid particular emphasis on solidarity between Member States: while membership is in Finland's own interest, it is in the Union's interest to defend and promote the interests of its members.

An efficient and secure Union

Finland's traditional trade relations and development might lead to the conclusion that the

---

EUROPEAN ORGANIZATIONS OF WHICH FINLAND IS A MEMBER
(since year. . .)

Nordic Council (1955)
Conference on /Organization of Security and Cooperation in Europe CSCE/OSCE (1975)
European Free Trade Association EFTA (1986; associate member 1961)
Council of Europe (1989)
Council of Baltic Sea States CBSS (1992)
North Atlantic Cooperation Council NACC (observer 1992)
Barents Euro-Arctic Council BEAC (1993)
NATO Partnership for Peace PfP (1994)
European Union (1995)
Western European Union WEU (observer 1995)
Arctic Council (1996)
Euro-Atlantic Partnership Council EAPC (successor of NACC, 1997)
Western European Armaments Group WEAG (observer 1997)

country is not among the most enthusiastic promoters of integration. On the one hand, its previous policy on integration, based on a strict avoidance of supranational arrangements and political commitment, might arouse the suspicion that neutrality still curbs Finland's enthusiasm for integration. On the other hand, one might argue that Finland barely had time to prepare for its new role before joining the Union: membership only began to be discussed as a possibility two years before the application was submitted, and it might have looked as if the Union was not very well known in the country.

Misgivings concerning the Finnish policy of neutrality emerged from the Commission's opinion on the country's membership application. The Commission feared that neutrality, even as newly defined, might prove an obstacle to Finland's full participation in the common foreign and security policy (CFSP) or even prompt it to hamper its implementation. The Commission required reassurance that Finland was prepared to accept the Union as an indivisible whole, including its progress towards a common defence policy.

Full acceptance of the Maastricht Treaty was thus a prerequisite of membership. The new Member States issued a separate declaration of assurance that they accepted the CFSP in full, including its defence policy dimension. In the end, foreign and security policy did not prove a stumbling block in the membership negotiations; the main problems were concerned with regional and agricultural policy.

Before joining, Finland did its homework well. The free movement of capital was implemented at the same time as in the EU, the Maastricht convergence criteria were adopted as economic policy guidelines, and the Finnish mark was tied to the ecu; the harmonization of laws had already been in progress for some time both nationally and in the context of Nordic cooperation. By the time that the EEA Agreement was signed, legislation concerning the single market had been harmonized. More-

■ Professor Jorma Routti is Director General of DG XII of the European Commission. The Directorate General for science, research and development, DG XII is in charge of the EU Framework Programmes for research and technological development and makes decisions on project grants.

Routti has taught at several universities in Finland and the universities of Geneva and Berkeley. Before being appointed to his current post in 1996, he served as director of SITRA, the Finnish National Fund for Research and Development.

over, Finland was on the same lines as the EU in many trade and foreign policy issues, as attested by its voting behaviour in the UN.

On the other hand, the Finns themselves also had their own suspicions of the EU. Some feared for the country's sovereignty, distinctive character and influence, while others claimed that these goals would actually be promoted and protected by EU membership. The overriding concerns, however, were the consequences of remaining outside and particularly the loss of all influence on decisions made within the Union.

The suspicions on both sides have proved unfounded. Finland has held its promise to participate fully in all Union activity, and the Finns have assessed the consequences of membership as primarily favourable.

■ ■ A key objective of Finland's EU policy is to define a new Northern dimension for the union. Much of the Baltic Sea is now surrounded by EU Member States, and among other coastal states Poland, Latvia, Lithuania and Estonia have applied for membership. The EU also wishes to support democratization and political stability in Russia and to promote utilization of the country's enormous natural resources.

Finland's membership is changing both Finland and the EU

Apart from introducing an unintelligible new language, Finland – together with Sweden – has brought a new, northern dimension to the European Union. The exotic farming conditions, rye fields, risk of night frost, rugged soil and sparse settlement explain the importance of regional and agricultural policy and the problems of reaching consensus – although the Europeanized Finns now process their rye into fresh pasta, no amount of EU aid can make all cereal crops thrive in the brief northern summer. Finland's membership has also brought the issues of northern security policy onto the EU's agenda. The EU now has over 1,200 kilometres of border with Russia.

Finland's influence could also be detected in the 1996–97 Intergovernmental Conference on completing and amending the Treaties of the European Union. The Treaty of Amsterdam, signed in October 1997, bears a Finnish stamp in its provisions on transparency, environment, employment and consumer protection. The Finnish representatives have been rather proud of the way their country has so quickly learned how things get done in the Union. The Treaty of Amsterdam is believed to have further strengthened Finland's position, by now as an 'established' Member State.

A Finnish imprint is also visible in the Union's foreign and defence policy. In accordance with a joint initiative of Sweden and Finland, the crisis management operations of Western European Union (WEU) were placed under the EU umbrella, i.e. the EU will use WEU to carry them out. At the same time, all EU Member States, including the nonaligned ones, were given an equal right to participate in planning and deciding on such operations.

The Finnish initiative on the "northern dimension" of the EU similarly seeks to strengthen the operational capability and external role of the Union. The idea is to establish a systematic northern policy and coordinate the work of international organizations operating in the area. The practical objectives are concerned with improving communications, developing infrastructure, and promoting economic relations and environmental protection. While the EU is expected to benefit, for example, from increased cooperation in the energy sector, the initiative also embraces the broader objective of increasing stability and furthering democracy and the market economy in Russia. Thus it is part of the general effort to integrate Russia into the system of western cooperation.

How, then, has EU membership affected Finland? Now that most Finnish policies are formulated within a broader context, Finland has new opportunities to act in international relations and to influence decisions that affect it. EU membership has substantial image value for Finland. The Union is seen as a community built on solidarity that strengthens Finland's international status

▼ Colza fields provide cheerful patches of colour in the Finnish landscape, but they are a sensitive issue in the European Union's talks on agriculture.

and, indirectly, also its security.

The principal reason for the success of Finland's EU policy has no doubt been its unshakeable pragmatism. Finland's foreign policy has always been determined primarily by practical considerations. Thus integration, too, is seen pragmatically, less as an ideal than as a form of cooperation with its own advantages and disadvantages. Nor are the Finns likely to have any overblown ideas about their own capacity or importance. They seek viable solutions by splitting large, complex issues into smaller ones more easily resolved. Finland also tends to focus on the areas that are most important to it and in which it can contribute special expertise, thereby preserving its credibility. This approach is backed by public opinion.

The Finnish approach to EU membership has also been explained by the lessons learned from the country's political history. Some say that Finland has learned political realism from belonging first to the powerful kingdom of Sweden and then to the Russian Empire, and after that living next to the Soviet Union. Others counter that Finland's commitment to a powerful EU is a way of emphasizing

that things have changed; the Finns now wish to be 'ordinary' Europeans – if indeed such a concept exists.

Thus EU membership has rapidly become central to Finnish foreign policy: it is a key factor of both our bilateral relations and our participation in multilateral international cooperation.

For Finland, the EU and NATO are the cornerstones of European cooperation and of the European security architecture. Finnish security policy focuses increasingly on cooperation and participation. In a speech delivered in early 1998, President Martti Ahtisaari defined Finnish security as being based on military nonalignment, an independent defence, EU membership, as well as on cooperation within the new NATO structures. Finland also seeks to intensify cooperation within all the major European organizations. While the EU is the most important of these, Finland also emphasizes the importance of WEU – in which it has had the status of observer since 1995 – and seeks closer contacts with NATO. According to Foreign Minister Tarja Halonen, Finland's recent actions prove that even a nonaligned country can play an important role in the field of security policy.

JACOB SÖDERMAN

■ The institution of the ombudsman derives from the Nordic countries. The position of parliamentary ombudsman was established in Finland by the Constitution Act of 1919. In the European Union, the right of citizens to make complaints to the ombudsman was introduced with the Treaty of Maastricht. The first European ombudsman, elected by the European Parliament in 1995, is Jacob Söderman, who previously held the same position in the Finnish Parliament. One of his major tasks to date was a report on how the European institutions apply the legal provisions on administrative transparency.

EU citizens and businesses registered in the Member States may submit complaints to the ombudsman concerning grievances related to the administration of the EU institutions or agencies.

After graduating in law, Jacob Söderman taught at university and worked for the Association of Finnish Local Authorities and the Ministry of Social Affairs and Health. He served in Finland as a Member of Parliament, Minister of Justice, Governor of Uusimaa Province and, for five years, as Parliamentary Ombudsman.

Finland seeks a form of security based on cooperation and guaranteeing stability, while promoting cooperation between the various organizations. The principles of the Organization for Security and Cooperation in Europe (OSCE), according to which states have the sovereign right to decide on their own security arrangements and in so doing have a duty to take account of the interests of others, are vital to Finland.

Relations with NATO are seen within the context of increasing dialogue and interaction in European security policy. Finland's role within the NATO structure began in 1992, when the country became an observer in the NACC, the North Atlantic Cooperation Council. Finland joined the NATO Partnership for Peace in 1994, and has been involved in the work of the NACC's successor, the Euro-Atlantic Council, since its founding in 1997. Finland has also taken part in NATO-led peacekeeping operations in Bosnia.

Although still nonaligned, Finland no longer rules out the possibility of joining a military alliance, even though the official position is that this is not the right moment to apply for NATO membership. As long as there is uncertainty about the interpretation that would be given to the political signals involved in alignment, Finland will seek to avoid making an outright choice. If a goal has been adopted, it is that of mitigating the difference between non-membership and membership in military alliances, and thus of preventing the emergence of new divisions.

Advocating an effective Union

Finland's EU policy is naturally dictated by national interests. On this basis, Finland takes an active part in developing the Union, and considers that it is in the Union's own interest to defend the interests of its members. Finland particularly emphasizes solidarity as the foundation of the EU's actions. The Union should be an open, democratic alliance of independent members, applying the pragmatic – and therefore desirable – principles of subsidiarity and proportionality.

At the same time, Finland supports an effective Union. Some have called the Finnish approach a mainstream policy; rather than pursuing sweeping visions of its own, the country seems to be content to follow the lead of others. It is thought to be an advantage for a small country to remain within the core of the Union; thus, the Finns have considered it particularly important to take part in EMU from the beginning. At the same time, the Union's modes of operation and internal unity need reinforcing. If the Union does not act effectively and commit its members sufficiently, in practice the large Member States may take the decisions out of the hands of the Community institutions, beyond the reach of the smaller members and joint supervision.

Finland also emphasizes effectiveness in another sense: once a decision has been taken, it should be carried out as effectively as possible – which also means that it must be possible to monitor its implementation. In true Nordic fashion, Finland is averse to making decisions for their own sake; it is taken as a matter of course that one should only set targets one intends to achieve. At the same time, the Finns emphasize the need for a clear, jointly agreed set of rules, giving all Member States an equal right to take part in formulating policies and deciding on objectives and schedules. The same goes for the further development of the common foreign and security policy. The Finnish position is that this requires a clear vision of the common goals and needs of the Member States. It is vital that the policy goals be clear to all, and that no Member State's interests be encroached upon. Finland's foreign policy thinking concurs in many respects with the CFSP: its main goals are to promote peace, security and human rights on the basis of unanimity, common interests and common values. These values include democracy, social justice and environmental stewardship.

Finland also supports further enlargement of the Union. Enlargement will increase stability in Finland's neighbouring areas. The Union is by nature a cooperative enterprise; it does not seek to assert its power in international relations, but to build links. The development of relations between Russia and the EU is particularly important to Finland, as are the efforts made to integrate Russia into the Western economic and legal system. In this respect, the Partnership Agreement between Russia and the EU, which came into force in December 1997, represents an important step forward.

Europe's many dimensions

Neighbourly relations with the other Nordic countries, Russia and the Baltic States are naturally just as important to Finland today as they were before joining the EU. The traditional 'northern dimension' of Finnish policy includes Nordic cooperation in its various forms; in recent years, it has also come to include cooperation in the Baltic Sea and Barents Sea regions and with nearby areas of the former Soviet Union.

The Nordic cooperation network has been a crucial factor facilitating Finland's adaptation to EU membership: joint Nordic efforts in the field of legislation in the 1980s focused in practice on following economic and legislative developments in the EC and thus making it easier for the Nordic countries to make the adjustments necessitated by European cooperation.

From a European perspective, it may sometimes be difficult to understand the nature of Nordic relations. The Nordic countries seem remarkably similar despite the fact that the Finnish language is so far removed from Swedish, for example; on the other hand, despite their similarity, the Nordic countries sometimes seem bent on emphasizing their differences. While presenting a united front in some issues, they sometimes prefer to assert their independence. Nordic relations are characterized by a measure of fraternal squabbling, an alternation of choral harmony and solo performances.

In their stance on major issues of European policy, such as EMU, the Nordic countries are often miles apart. On some questions, they may pursue similar goals, but at different times and in different ways. Core issues, however, have always brought the importance of cooperation to the fore; thus, all Nordic countries insisted on a special arrangement permitting Norway and Iceland to join the Schengen Agreement on free mobility in order to ensure the continuity of the Nordic passport union, which goes back to the 1950s.

Reconciling the Nordic and West European models of cooperation and integration has provided new impetus for developing Nordic cooperation; on the other hand, the well-established 'Nordic model' could well yield new ideas for cooperation within the EU.

In many respects, Nordic cooperation has attained the gener-

▼ A poster published in all 15 Member States for Europe Day, May 9.

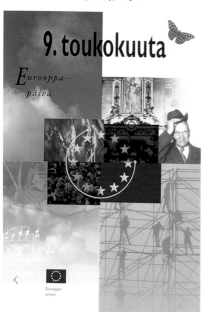

al acceptance and legitimacy that the EU aspires to. The Nordic countries have often been heard to speak 'in one voice' at international conferences, and they have had a joint representation in many organizations for decades now. Such legitimacy does not arise overnight; it requires broad-based and prolonged cooperation. Meetings between Nordic ministers have been arranged on a regular basis since the 1930s and, at a more informal level, Nordic cooperation has always included extensive contacts between non-governmental organizations. The Nordic Council and the Nordic Council of Ministers have coordinated such contacts rather than creating them, acting closer to national governments than most similar organizations. The well-established principle of free movement of persons, a focus on cultural and linguistic contacts, and cross-border cooperation between regional and local authorities are of particular interest in the EU context, as are the Nordic countries' actions to stimulate links with neighbouring areas of Russia and the Baltic States and the Baltics' increasing participation in joint Nordic affairs.

Relations with Russia and the Baltic States represent an important aspect of the northern dimension for Finland. Russo-Finnish relations have changed somewhat in the wake of Finland's EU membership, primarily by taking on a new, multilateral dimension. During recent visits of the Finnish president to Russia, the media have noted that the visitor is not representing merely Finland but also the whole Union.

Significant changes were made to the contractual basis of bilateral relations between Russia and Finland in the early 1990s. In autumn 1991 Finland started parallel negotiations on a new agreement with both the Soviet Union and the Russian Federation; the former disintegrated in December 1991, and the new agreement on good neighbourly relations was eventually signed with Russia in January 1992. At the same time, the YYA agreement was rescinded. The new agreement no longer contains any provisions on defence obligations or consultations; it bans the use or threat of force in relations between the two countries and encourages direct contacts and cooperation between authorities, NGOs and citizens. The agreement stresses the basic principles of international relations, such as respect for human rights and the fundamental freedoms, and emphasizes the market economy, European values and environmental protection.

If EU membership, as it were, reduced the distance between Finland and Europe, Finland and Russia have also drawn closer together. Trade relations between the two countries have evolved from bilateral clearing trade to normal business-to-business transactions; official, top-down cooperation and strict control of travel have given way to grassroots activity and spontaneous exchanges between private organizations and citizens, by commerce and tourism. All in all, relations between the two countries have been normalized, or "Europeanized", as President Ahtisaari put it in a 1997 speech in Moscow.

In order to further Russian integration into Western economic and political cooperation, Finland is seeking, on the one hand, to extend agreements between Russia and Western organizations, and on the other to help connect Rus-

▲ Finland has participated in UN peace-keeping operations primarily in the Middle East, but also in Cyprus and former Yugoslavia. Finnish SFOR troops in Bosnia-Herzegovina.

towards democracy and market economy. Within the UN, Finland has sometimes been called a superpower of peacekeeping; the country has a long and acclaimed history in the field, and together with the other Nordic countries has always been a staunch supporter of the world organization.

Finland is a member of numerous overlapping and interrelated international organizations. The wide range of Nordic organizations has been of particular value for the whole of Europe. It includes the Nordic Council and Nordic Ministerial Council, the Council of Baltic Sea States, the Arctic Council and the Council of the Barents Euro-Arctic Region, as well as several specialized joint organizations and forums. The Barents Sea Council also meets as a regional body with delegates from the local governments of the northernmost regions of its member states. The involvement of regional administrations, ethnic minorities and indigenous peoples is in fact an important aspect of Nordic cooperation. These organizations also provide an extensive network for the development of infrastructure, cooperation in energy matters and other interaction. The Finnish 'northern dimension' initiative seeks to make use of this network and to promote EU participation in the development of the region.

The Council of Baltic Sea States, the Arctic Council and the Barents Council have another special characteristic that makes them valuable forums even in a broader context. In practice, they bring to the same table the important countries and groups of countries that are only seen to be geographically close viewed from

sia with the West via a policy of small, practical steps, enlarging the interface between Western and Russian society by developing environmental, educational and commercial relations.

At the same time, Finland is promoting closer integration of the Central and Eastern European states, and especially the Baltic states, into Western cooperation. Good relations between the Baltics and Russia are naturally an important factor in this, and Finland attaches importance to their promotion in forums such as the OSCE.

For many years now, the OSCE and the UN have occupied a special position in Finnish foreign policy. The OSCE has also offered a forum for the development of transatlantic relations, crisis prevention and management, and the peaceful transition

a northern perspective. While Russia is a member of all three councils, the United States and Canada are members of the Arctic Council and, together with many EU Member States and Japan, observers in the Barents Council. Meanwhile, Poland and several EU countries have observer status in the Arctic Council. Thus northern cooperation brings together all the major powers including Japan, as well as the countries of Europe in the broadest sense, from Iceland to Italy and from the Baltics to the United Kingdom. The European Union itself is a member of both the Council of Baltic Sea States and the Barents Council.

tions between the EU and Russia is vital to Finland. The opportunity to influence this development as the presiding Member State and decisions on how to maintain the momentum of rapprochement represent a tremendous challenge for Finland. The *Ostpolitik* of the EU is based on the idea that stability in Russia guarantees peace in Europe. This stability is promoted by progress towards a democratic political system and market economy; thus, full support must be given to integrating Russia into the glo-

▼ Foreign Minister Tarja Halonen is a lawyer by training. She has previously held the posts of Second Minister for Social Affairs and Health and Minister of Justice. Here, Minister Halonen shows a T-shirt she bought for President Ahtisaari at a conference for women.

The challenges of EU Presidency

Finland took up the Presidency of the Council of the European Union for the first time in the second half of 1999. Outgoing Commission President Jacques Santer has expressed his hope that a whole new political dimension to the Union can be introduced under Finnish leadership. The establishment of political partnership with Russia is particularly important to the Union, and many feel that Finland may be better equipped to handle this than any other Member State.

In many ways, Finland is genuinely between East and West; it is a country of two official languages, two national churches and several officially recognized minorities, with a culture that is undeniably a hybrid of western, northern and eastern elements. The smooth development of rela-

LOOK AT THE WORLD THROUGH WOMEN'S EYES

bal economy and promoting its participation in European cooperation. In its bilateral relations with Russia, Finland has benefited in many ways from EU membership, which has not only stimulated Finnish practical initiatives with the help of various aid programmes, but has also increased Finland's attractiveness to Russia as a trading partner.

Finland is expected to contribute its expertise on Russia and an active approach to improving relations. But how much chance does it really have of linking Europe's western and eastern dimensions? There is no standard procedure to follow. Although Finland has always been part of Europe, it is now redefining its own Europeanness. The EU is not the whole continent, but it is very tangibly organizing Europe in a new way; this is also seen in the reformulation of Finland's relations with other European states. And even though Finland has always been Russia's neighbour, like other countries it is now starting anew, rebuilding its specific knowledge of and its relations with Russia.

With a policy based on small steps to advance cooperation, highlighting the northern dimension and actively defining the EU's relations with Russia, Finland seems to be assuming the offered role, helping to break down the divisions of the Cold War and increasing concrete contacts between Russia and the EU.

The Presidency will represent a challenge to such a small country. Finland will adopt a general European approach rather than a pronouncedly 'northern' attitude. It has generally been considered that small countries can handle the Presidency quite effectively, lacking as they do the national ambitions of the larger Member States, and are thus perhaps better able than others to mediate between conflicting views and to negotiate decisions. The intrinsic pragmatism of the Finns should help. The Presidency will also offer Finland a prime opportunity to deepen its relations with the other Member States and with the Community institutions, to which the country will look for assistance and guidance.

A Land
of Many Faces

Finland is a place with a character all its own, where East and West merge. The history, culture and religion of the country set the Finns squarely among the peoples of Western Europe; and yet the eastern influence is strong. A similar contrast characterizes the Finnish landscape. Southern Finland features groves of deciduous trees such as oak, while the central region is dotted with lakes and conifer forests, and the north is a land of bare fells, open expanses and dwarf birch.

A varied landscape

A sparsely populated country in the far northeastern corner of Europe, Finland is nevertheless a mid-sized European state in terms of land area. Almost one quarter of the country's territory lies north of the Arctic Circle, making Finland the world's northernmost country together with Iceland. In the south and west, Finland is bounded by the Baltic Sea, offering a direct sea route to the Continent. The broken coastline in the southwest gradually gives way to the Saaristomeri, or Archipelago Sea, unique in the world for the multitude, variety and closeness of its islands. All in all, Finland's territorial waters count over 80,000 islands, the two largest being the main island of the Åland group and Kemiö, just southeast of Turku.

Finland lies on the western fringe of the Eurasian boreal coniferous zone, the *taiga*. The forests are characterized by a paucity of species: the only trees of any economic significance are pine, spruce, birch and, to a lesser extent, alder and aspen. Although Finland extends from the northern boundary of the oak zone to the bare subarctic fells, the country has no mountain ranges proper. The highest altitudes are in the country's northwestern 'arm', the Enontekiö region, an outlier of the Scandic fells featuring Finland's highest peak Haltiatunturi (or Halti, 1328 metres).

The lie of the land is characterized by small-scale variation. Most of the country is low-lying, and slopes gently towards the south or southeast. Eastern Finland is dotted with lakes and high hills; the rolling landscape of Central Finland gives way in the west to the

▶ The Finnish landscape is dotted with lakes, islands and forests.

Ostrobothnian plains, with hillocks and lowlands in other coastal areas. The bare, rugged fells of Lapland are separated by canyons gouged by turbulent rivers.

The topography is founded on the ancient bedrock, most of which was formed some 1 800–1 900 million years ago. In contrast, the soil is very young, for the glaciers of the last Ice Age carried off virtually all loose matter. A reminder of this relatively recent period of glaciation is the uplift phenomenon, which continues to remodel the landscape, increasing the country's land area by some 7 square kilometres every year.

Finland has something like 188,000 lakes, more than almost any other country in the world. Lakes constitute about 10 per cent of Finland's total area; indeed, in some parts of the country a quarter or even half of the surface is under water. Most of the lakes are very small, but the largest, Greater Saimaa, ranks fourth in Europe and forty-third in the world.

The rivers are mostly short and have a relatively small discharge, as none of the watersheds are far from the coast. The principal watershed is called Maanselkä, which separates the rivers running into the Baltic Sea (91%) from those discharging into the Arctic Ocean and the White Sea (9%). The longest river is Kemijoki-Kitinen (552 km).

The aquatic environment is unique. The smooth-worn bedrock, the Ice Age and uplift have together created a veritable maze of waterways. The large lakes of central Finland are virtually at the same altitude. Between them meanders an

◀ Finland's four seasons.

endless succession of narrows and slow-flowing straits, interspersed with inlets, headlands and islands. The lakes contain a total of nearly 100,000 islands, the second highest number in the world after Canada.

Some 70% of the land area is productive forest, making Finland the most densely forested country in Europe. The proportion of mires is higher than anywhere else in the world. If poor-growth forest is included, wetlands represent almost one third of Finland's territory.

Finland's fauna is similar to that of Scandinavia and northern Russia, consisting mostly of species typical of the boreal coniferous zone, such as the brown bear, the national animal. In addition, arctic species are found in the north and typical European species in the south. The fauna have arrived so recently that few species are endemic, a rare exception being the ringed seal of Saimaa, a protected species that is a relict from the post-glacial era.

▶ During the last glacial epoch, the ringed seal was cut off from the sea and stranded in the Lake Saimaa water system. It is an endangered species today, its survival threatened mainly by motorboats and fishermen's nets, in which the seals often become entangled.

In February 1996, the biggest snow castle in the world was inaugurated in the town of Kemi in northern Finland. It featured over 400 metres of walls and an auditorium with seating for 1 500 spectators. More than 270 000 people came to see it that winter, and the town decided to build a new castle every year to attract winter tourists and to serve as a cultural centre. The people kept coming, and by spring 1999 the visitor count was over a million people from 74 countries. The first two castles were sponsored by UNICEF, and from 1998 to 2000 the Finnish Red Cross is Kemi's partner in the venture. The secret to the castle's success is its uniqueness and potential for innovation. Since the

castle has to be built from scratch every year, there is plenty of scope for technical experimentation, while the builders learn from past years' experience. The University of Oulu's engineering department is involved in the project, studying the behaviour of snow and ice constructions at changing temperatures.

West wind, polar night and midnight sun

The Finnish climate is a great deal milder than might be expected given the northern location of the country. The cold is moderated by the Baltic Sea, the inland waters and, above all, the westerly winds bringing in Atlantic air warmed by the Gulf Stream.

The mean temperature in Finland is between 6°C and 10°C higher than elsewhere in the world at similar latitudes.

The winters are relatively humid and cold. The occasional continental fronts that push in from the east cause severe frosts in the winter and heat waves in the summer. During the coldest winters the temperature in the north may fall to –40°C or even –50°C, whereas readings of up to +35°C have been recorded during

▲ ▼ For centuries, travellers have been drawn to Lapland to marvel at the midnight sun. More recent innovations are polar night tours and visits to Father Christmas' home region. Above, the midnight sun stains the whole sky a yellowish red. Below, the moon provides the only relief to the gloom of the polar night.

the brief summer. Many visitors find the sharp seasonal shifts hard to get used to.

Winter is the longest season in Finland. In northernmost Lapland, the polar night, or *kaamos*, lasts 52 days, while the southern parts of the country have just six hours of daylight in the darkest midwinter period. The light of summer makes up for the winter darkness. On the south coast, the sun is up for almost 19 hours at midsummer. In Nuorgam in the far north, the sun does not set for 67 days. Although rain or snow falls throughout the year, overall precipitation is not evenly divided. The early summer tends to be too dry for the farmers' liking, especially in the southwest and along the Ostrobothnian coast, whereas rainfall is often excessive at the end of the growing season (the period during which the average daily temperature exceeds 5°C). This season lasts about two months longer in the south than in the north, although the difference is offset somewhat by the fact that Lapland's midnight sun provides plants with a larger daily dose of light during the summer.

Natural resources and the environment

Finland has a wealth of natural resources in terms of both raw materials and sources of energy. Most of these – including the most important resource, wood – are renewable. Finland's overall forest reserves (1900 million cubic metres) are Europe's fourth largest after Russia, Sweden and Germany. Annual forest growth amounts to almost 75 million cubic metres. Another major resource is water, which is used by both households and industry, and as a source of energy.

PUBLIC RIGHT OF ACCESS IN FINLAND

■ Public right of access (the Finnish term *jokamiehenoikeus* means "everyman's right") means that every citizen has access to the land, regardless of who owns it. You don't have to ask the owner for permission to enter his land, and normally don't have to pay a fee either. Naturally you mustn't damage the owner's property or disturb his peace. On the Finnish mainland, this right comprises:

– the right of access on foot, on skis, or by bicycle; off limits are courtyards, fields, meadows and planted areas susceptible to damage; camping at a reasonable distance from habitation is permitted;
– the right to pick wild berries, mushrooms and flowers, as long as they are not protected species;
– the right of access to water for boating, bathing and washing; the right to travel over ice.

The rules in the Åland Islands differ from those on the mainland on a few points: certain rights available to everyone on the mainland are restricted in Åland to permanent residents.

▶ Oulankajoki National Park near Kuusamo is a paradise for hikers, especially when the autumn colours are at their height.

◀ ▼ The swan and the bear are national symbols.

Non-renewable resources derive from inorganic nature. Finland's bedrock contains many rock types suitable for use as industrial raw material. Ore resources are also varied; even some promising diamond and gold deposits have been discovered in recent years. The most valuable non-renewable resources are gravel, sand, clay and peat (classified as non-renewable because it takes so long to form).

The environment is exceptionally intact and unpolluted. Nevertheless, the Finns have been paying increasing attention to conservation in the last few years. The most important sector of environmental protection is water conservation. Most of the pollutants released into the environment eventually wind up in the waters. In Finland these are shallow and thus easily contaminated. Observations indicate that the acidification of lakes in southern Finland finally came to a halt in 1996, while air quality has improved since the 1970s. Half of the overall air pollution is caused by indigenous sources, while the other half consists of transboundary pollution.

There is a wide variety of nature conservation areas, and the most important are classified as nature reserves or national parks. Visitors need a special permit to enter one of the 19 nature reserves. The 32 national parks serve the purposes of research, education and recreation. Various biotopes, such as bogs, waters, tundra and forests are protected in the national parks. There are also special conservation areas for wetlands, deciduous groves, shores and old-growth forests.

In accordance with the EU nature and bird directives, the goal of the Natura 2000 conservation programme is to ensure the preservation of biodiversity in the Euroean Union. The programme protects 12 per cent of Finland's area.

Population

The Finns' forefathers first came to the shores of Finland some time between 9000 and 8000 B.C. They found a barren coastline, laid waste by the retreating continental ice shelf. The settlers arrived from at least two different directions, east

NATIONAL CHARACTER
■ Zachris Topelius (1818–1898) was the best-known portrayer of his country and its people, and has had perhaps a stronger influence than anyone else on the way the Finns perceive themselves. According to Topelius, the Finnish national character could be summed up in four words: cautious, stubborn, taciturn and imperturbable. All these qualities stem directly from Finland's stark nature.

Blond hair and blue eyes are often thought of as typically Finnish features. According to a rough estimate, three quarters of the Finns' genetic makeup is of Baltic-Germanic origin and one quarter of Eastern origin.

▲ The Lapps still don their colourful traditional costumes.

and south. Finland has remained settled ever since that time. Over the centuries, new waves of settlers arrived from different directions, but they were all assimilated into the earlier population.

Extremely sparsely settled for many centuries, Finland has seen a prolonged period of population growth in the 20th century. The population first surpassed three million in 1914 and attained four million in 1950. As a result of the postwar baby boom, the population reached four and a half million by 1965. Around this time, the birth rate sagged, and what with mass emigration to Sweden in search of jobs, the population actually decreased in 1969 and 1970.

Population growth picked up somewhat in the 1980s, as many emigrants returned and the birth rate increased. The five-million mark was reached in 1991, and by spring 1999 Finland had a population of 5,159,646. Demographically, the country is characterized by a high proportion of working-age people and a steadily aging population. Children (0 to 14) account for less than one fifth of the population, while the proportion of senior citizens (over 65s) is now over 16%. Over two thirds of the Finns are in the working-age category (15 to 64).

Over 51% of the country's population are women. This is primarily due to a higher mortality rate among men; more boys are born than girls. Women account for more than two thirds of the senior citizens category.

The population is unusually homogeneous, as the only indigenous ethnic minorities are the Sámi of Lapland and the Romany. The majority of the former (a group of from 3000 to 6000 people, depending on the criteria applied) live in the Sámi home region in the northernmost municipalities of Lapland, while the 9000-strong Romany population are more evenly distributed throughout the country.

The proportion of foreigners is among the lowest in Europe. At the end of 1998, a bare 85,060 foreign citizens were living in Finland. The number of immigrants from the former Soviet Union, however, has grown rapidly in recent years. The country has received only a limited number of refugees, some 15,500 in all. In 1997, 973 persons applied for asylum in Finland.

▼ In Finland's bilingual communities, street names and road signs are in both Finnish and Swedish.

The official languages are Finnish and Swedish; Sámi has official status within the Sámi home region. Finnish, a language belonging to the Finno-Ugric family, holds an uncontested dominant position, being the mother tongue of over 93% of the population. Fewer than 6% of the Finns speak Swedish as their mother tongue; most of them live on the south or west coast or in the Åland Islands.

Finnish is a very distinctive language and the only non-Indo-European language of the European Union. It is characterized by fine shades of meaning sometimes hard to pin down precisely, and an affinity for natural phenomena, with many onomatopoeic words for natural sounds. Perhaps because of this 'different' quality of the language, no satisfactory translation has ever been produced of the greatest and the most Finnish of all Finnish novels, Aleksis Kivi's nineteenth-century masterpiece *The Seven Brothers*. Few people outside the country's borders speak Finnish, but the language can be studied at more than 70 universities abroad today.

Irregular settlement

Finland is Europe's third most sparsely populated country after Iceland and Norway. The population density at the beginning of 1998 was 16.9 persons per square kilometre. Although the country is settled throughout, the population density varies greatly. The principal city and capital is Helsinki, which has 546,317 inhabitants (1999). About 920,000 people live in the Helsinki Metropolitan Area, which includes

the neighbouring agglomerations of Espoo, Vantaa and Kauniainen. This functionally coherent capital region can be compared with the similar regions of Stockholm, Oslo and Copenhagen.

The third largest city after Helsinki and Espoo is Tampere, the largest inland settlement in the Nordic countries. Turku, Finland's capital until 1812, is currently the fifth largest city (Vantaa being no. 4).

▲ Helsinki is known as the White City of the North. Here, the city centre as seen from the sea. The Swedish Embassy in the centre, with the Cathedral dome soaring high above it. In the foreground Kauppatori, the main market.

Rising housing standards

Housing is an even more vital requirement in the north than in milder climates. The Finn's life centres on the home and its immediate surroundings. Much of the housing stock was replaced during the construction boom of the 1970s and '80s, while in the 1990s the focus shifted to renovation and refurbishment. Compared with other European countries, Finnish housing is new and of high quality.

Most Finns would prefer to live in a house of their own, surrounded by a private garden. Large-scale construction of single-family houses, however, only really got under way in the late 1970s. Today there are almost as many single-family homes as flats: both account for over 40% of total housing, while other low-rise housing, such as terraced houses and rowhouses, accounts for 12%.

Urbanization came late to Finland, and a large part of the population still long for the peace and quiet of the country. Many are therefore willing to make do with a cramped apartment in the city to be able to afford a summer cottage of their own. There are nearly 400,000 such second homes in Finland, most of them on the coast or by a lakeside.

Another obligatory feature of Finnish housing is the sauna bath, of which there are 1.3 million in the country. The sauna is sacred to the Finns; its significance might be compared with that of the tea ceremony to the Japanese. Every block of flats, even every individual house – not to speak of summer cottages

Tourism

Finland is too far north to ever become a target for mass tourism. Its main attractions are a safe, stable social fabric, sparse settlement and untouched nature. Whereas in most countries landowners may prevent or restrict entry to their land with fences and notices, in Finland there are few restrictions to access: you are free to wander at will and gather native ber-

▲ Life without a sauna, a sanctuary for physical and mental relaxation, would be unthinkable for the Finns. The best saunas are built on the waterfront.

– must have its own sauna. Bathing in a sauna has an incomparable cleansing and relaxing effect, especially when accompanied by a dip in cool water. In the winter, the hardiest bathers sometimes roll in the snow to cool off.

ries, mushrooms and flowers even on private land.

Finland provides a rich range of culture, nature and adventure tourism. Myriad summer music events offer the finest international quality in authentic Finnish settings, the three most famous being the Savonlinna Opera Festival, the Kuhmo Chamber Music Festival and the Pori Jazz Festival. Vast forests and winding waterways provide excellent opportunities for adventure tourism, often arranged by companies for their staff, and give hikers, canoeists and fishing enthusi-

asts inexhaustible opportunities to explore and test their survival skills. Thousands of well-fitted holiday homes provide the perfect opportunity for relaxation and privacy far from the city crowds. Finland's fifty-odd

▲ Snowmobile and husky safaris are among Lapland's biggest tourist attractions.

NORTHERN LIGHTS

■ The Northern lights (or aurora borealis) are an optical phenomenon occurring most frequently near the magnetic poles. They arise when electrically charged particles powered by the solar wind and travelling at great speed collide with atoms and molecules in the atmosphere. The collision excites these atoms and molecules, which emit a photon as they discharge.

The usual colour of the Northern lights is yellowish green, emitted by oxygen atoms generally some 90 to 150 kilometres above the earth's surface. The red aurora occasionally sighted above the green also stems from oxygen atoms, while ionized nitrogen molecules emit blue and purple light. The aurora borealis occurs in both summer and winter, but in the summer it never gets dark enough for the lights to be visible. In Finland you are likeliest to get a glimpse of the aurora on a late winter evening in northern Lapland, but from time to time they shine brightly in the southern parts of the country, too.

The main centre for research on the Northern lights is in Sodankylä.

▲ As almost everyone knows, Father Christmas lives in Finland, setting out in Rudolph the Red-Nosed Reindeer's sleigh to distribute presents to all the world's children.

full-size golf courses offer visitors the magic of natural light around the clock in summer.

Finland's reputation as a winter holiday destination has grown steadily. The main attractions are cross-country and Alpine skiing, snowboarding, snowmobile safaris and husky-drawn sleighrides. The popularity of many winter resorts is enhanced by spas of high standard; indeed, Finland is the leading Nordic country in terms of the number of bathing resorts. The largest numbers of visitors come from Sweden and Russia; the Germans are the third biggest tourist group in Finland.

In dark December, tourists are drawn to Finland by the one and only genuine Father Christmas. About 40,000 visitors, great and small, travel from Britain alone to see him. With the rapid increase in his popularity, Father Christmas has continually enlarged his domain. Santapark, an underground amusement park near the Santa Claus Workshop Village on the Arctic Circle, opened at the end of 1998.

Finland is also a popular congress country, not least because many meetings between the world's leaders here have shown that the Finns are capable organizers of safe, smoothly functioning, high-profile international events. Approximately 200 international conferences are held in the country every year, attracting a total of over 50,000 participants, many of whom travel with a companion. Excellent transport connections ensure that a conference in Finland can easily be combined with a holiday in some other part of the country or in Russia or one of the Baltic countries. The car ferries operating between Sweden and Finland are real "floating hotels" and a major attraction in their own right.

Finland through the Centuries

Finland in the kingdom of Sweden

Until the twelfth century, Finland was a religious and political hinterland, coveted by its western neighbour Sweden and the Catholic Church on the one hand, and by its eastern neighbour the Principality of Novgorod (later Russia) and the Orthodox Church on the other. In 1155 or thereabouts the Swedes made a military expedition, later known as the First Crusade, to the southwest coast of Finland, which gave them a base for spreading the Christian religion and consolidating their secular power. In 1238 the Swedes strengthened their hold on Finland with the Second Crusade, taking them far inland into the region of Häme.

The eastern border Is drawn

With the Swedes tightening their grip on western Finland, Novgorod pushed in from the east to the region of Karelia. Alarmed by this development, Sweden embarked on its Third Crusade in 1293, reaching the mouth of the Gulf of Finland and building a fortress at Viipuri (Wiborg). Thus Sweden had won the race for the conquest of Finland. The Treaty of Pähkinäsaari (Schlüsselburg, today Petrokrepost) established the border between Sweden and Novgorod, leaving only the eastern part of Karelia to the latter.

Thus western and southern Finland came within the sphere of influence of West European culture, whereas the Russo-Byzantine culture

▼ King Erik of Sweden set off on his first crusade to Finland with the Scottish-born Bishop Henry around 1155. Henry stayed behind in Finland to convert and baptize the pagan Finns. According to legend, the farmer Lalli attacked and killed Henry on the ice of a frozen lake. The picture shows St. Henry surrounded by holy men, with his murderer prostrate at his feet.

▲ Construction of Turku Castle began in the late thirteenth century and continued for many centuries. The castle's heyday came during the Renaissance in the 1560s, when Duke John and his spouse Catharine Iagellonica held court there.

▼ King Gustav Vasa of Sweden confiscated the property of the Catholic Church throughout the country and ordered his subjects to convert to Lutheranism. This sketch by Albert Edelfelt shows Mikael Agricola, who studied under the tuition Martin Luther and eventually became Bishop of Finland, presenting his Finnish translation of the New Testament to the king.

▲ Finland's first university, The Academy of Turku was founded in 1640.

left its imprint on the eastern parts of the country. The annexed Finnish provinces became known in Sweden as "the Eastland," a name first recorded in the 1340s. The principal town of this region and the bishop's see was Turku, founded in the mid thirteenth century.

As part of Sweden, the Finns had some say in the affairs of the nation. In the 1362, they were granted the right to take part in the election of the king, and they also sent representatives to the Diet of Estates. At the end of the Middle Ages (in the early years of the sixteenth century), Finland had a population of some 350,000. Most of these were small farmers; even the largest towns were still of very modest size.

Gustavus Vasa ascended to the Swedish throne in 1523. He pursued a dual policy of increasing both the power and the revenues of the Crown. The Reformation, started just before this in Germany by Martin Luther, suited the royal plans perfectly, and so the Church of Rome rapidly lost its position to Lutheranism. The Reformation marked the beginning of the cultural role of vernacular languages. Mikael Agricola, Bishop of Turku and the father of written Finnish, translated numerous works into the vernacular, including the New Testament (1548). The full text of the Bible was first published in Finnish almost a century later, in 1642.

Splendour and misery of a great power

In the seventeenth century, Sweden expanded its territory around the whole Baltic Sea, pushing the eastern border of Finland further east as a result. Sweden's heyday was a time of wholesale progress in Finland, but it also meant increasingly centralized rule, as Stockholm tightened its administrative grip on the provinces. As it expanded, Sweden was obliged to strain its forces to the utmost. For its constant wars, the mother country conscripted an endless stream of Finnish soldiers. The province's misery was compounded by the famine of 1696 and 1697, when hunger and disease killed nearly one third of Finland's population.

Sweden's position as a great power came to an end with the disastrous war of 1700–1721, known as the

Great Northern War. The Russians occupied Finland during this war, but in the Treaty of Uusikaupunki (Nystad) in 1721 all the Finnish provinces except for the southeastern part of the country reverted to Sweden. Despite intermittent wars with Russia after this, the eighteenth century brought Finland an increase in population and economic improvement. Indeed, the population soared from 306,000 in the 1720s to 907,000 in 1807.

Industrialization got off to a cautious start with the founding of a handful of factories, including a glassworks, a sugar refinery and a paper mill. The most important industry at the time, however, was the production of sawn goods. Finland exported planks, tar and ships, and imported grain and salt as well as luxuries such as tobacco and coffee.

The first Finnish-language newspaper was founded in 1776. Many a leading scholar taught at the Academy of Turku, which had been founded back in 1640. Pehr Kalm, professor of economics, became famous for his journey to North America; Johan Gadolin, professor of chemistry, discovered a new group of elements, and Henrik Gabriel Porthan, professor of Latin and polymath, was the first to study Finnish language, history and poetry.

Grand Duchy of the Russian Empire

A new leaf in Finnish history was turned in winter 1808, as Russia declared war on Sweden and invaded Finland. The War of Finland, as this conflict is known, ended in Sweden's defeat, and in the peace treaty of 1809 Sweden ceded Finland to Russia. Thus almost seven centuries

▼ Tsar Alexander I opened the first Diet of Finland in 1809, raising Finland "to the rank of nations". Painting by Emanuel Thelning.

of Swedish rule in Finland had come to an end.

Russia awarded its newly-annexed province the status of a grand duchy. The Tsar of Russia was thus also Grand Duke of Finland, and his representative in the country was the Governor-General. The laws enacted during the Swedish period remained in force, and the Lutheran Church retained its leading position. The grand duchy was endowed with an administration of its own, with Swedish as the language of government. This extensive autonomy made Finland a unique entity of the Russian Empire, in effect a state within a state. The supreme executive body was the Senate (a kind of Government), whose members were all Finns. The Senate submitted decisions directly to the Tsar, past the Russian ministers and civil service.

The Russians did not think Turku a suitable capital for the grand duchy, as it was both culturally and geographically too close to Sweden. Helsinki was therefore made the capital of Finland by imperial decree in 1812.

Period of reform

Alexander I died in 1825 and was succeeded by Nicholas I. Although a reactionary ruler, the "Soldier Tsar" upheld Finland's autonomy. It was in fact under his rule that the nationalist Finnish movement began to gain momentum. The *Kalevala*, compiled by Elias Lönnrot and soon hailed as the Finnish national epic, was published in 1835; J.L. Runeberg, "the national poet" (who wrote in Swedish), produced a series of patriotic ballads.

J.V. Snellman, philosopher and senator, demanded that Finnish should replace Swedish as the language of the civil service and the educated class. The liberal

Väinämöinen kuvaa tiedoissa ja tuota kuvaisiksi; 1—30.

aka vanha Väinämöinen
Elelevi aikojansa
Noilla Väinölän ahoilla,
Kalevalan kankahilla,
Laulelevi virsiänsä,
Laulelevi, taitelevi.
   Lauloi päivät pääksytysten,
Yhytysten yöt saneli
Muinaisia muisteloita,
Noita syntyjä syviä,
Joit' ei laula kaikki lapset,
Ymmärrä yhet urohot
Tällä inhalla iällä,
Katovalla kannikalla.
   Kauas kuuluvi sanoma,
Ulos viestit vierähtävät
Väinämöisen laulannasta,
Urohon osoannasta,
Viestit vierähti suvehen,
Sai sanomat Pohjolahan.

◀ "Deep matters" (knowledge and wisdom) are treated in the *Kalevala*, the Finnish national epic.

▲ It was largely Johan Vilhelm Snellman's doing that the Grand Duchy of Finland was granted its own currency, the *markka*, in 1860. This marked a major step on the road to full independence from Russia.

▼ Tsar Nicholas II appointed Nikolai Bobrikov Governor-General of Finland in 1898 and charged him with the task of "Russifying" the province. The February Manifesto aimed at suppressing Finland's right to its own laws. Almost 530 000 Finns signed an appeal to the Tsar, and 1050 European scientists and scholars signed "the European Address Pro Finlandia". The Tsar did not acknowledge either address. Shown here is the highly decorated first page of the Swedish address.

Alexander II, who became Tsar in 1855, issued the "Language Manifesto" in 1863, according to which Finnish should be accorded equal status with Swedish as a language of the civil service and courts of law within twenty years. Nonetheless, Swedish retained its dominant position until the early years of the twentieth century.

Alexander I had convened the first Finnish Diet in 1809, but the Diet did not meet again until 1863. From that time, however, it was convened regularly, resulting in a whole spate of new legislation. The country's local government was overhauled, an elementary school system was introduced, and the 1878 Act on National Service founded a separate Finnish Army. Finland had already been given its own currency, the mark (*markka* in Finnish), in 1860.

Russification

The rise of Nicholas II to the throne in 1894 meant an increase in the influence of Russian ultra-nationalists. The Grand Duchy of Finland was a part of the Empire, to be sure, but sheltered by extensive privileges, and thus a thorn in their flesh. The "Russification" of Finland – that is, the eradication of what they saw as Finnish separatism – began during the "First Oppression" from 1899 to 1905, and continued during the "Second Oppression" from 1909 to 1917.

The Revolution of 1905 gave the Finns a brief respite, during which they managed to enact a new Constitution replacing the old Diet of Four Estates with a unicameral Parliament elected by universal suffrage applying to all men and women aged 24 or more. This was the most democratic national assembly in Europe at the time.

The Independent Republic

The First World War, which broke out in summer 1914, led to revolution in Russia in 1917. The February Revolution resulted in the deposition of the Tsar, and the October Revolution brought the Bolsheviks to power. Breaking with the revolutionary regime, the Finnish Parliament, in which the right-wing parties had the majority, proclaimed itself the supreme authority in Finland on November 15. With its newly-assumed powers, Parliament appointed a new Senate (Government) under P.E. Svinhufvud. Finland proclaimed itself independent on the basis of the Senate's proposal on December 6, 1917.

In the wake of the Bolshevik uprising in Russia, the gap between right and left also widened in Finland, soon reaching unbridgeable proportions. The situation was aggravated by the continued presence of some 70,000 Russian soldiers in Finland in early 1918. At the end of January, the extreme left and the Red Guard rebelled, and the Senate was forced to flee Helsinki. In the ensuing civil war, the Senate received assistance from Germany, while the rebels were aided by Soviet Russia. The war ended in mid-May 1918 in victory for the Senate troops under General C.G.E. Mannerheim.

Building the Republic

At the close of the civil war, the plan was to make Finland a monarchy with a German king, but following the collapse of Germany in November 1918, Finland had to shift its political allegiance westwards, and adopted a republican form of government. K.J. Ståhlberg was elected first President of the Republic in summer 1919.

Construction of the new independent republic now got under way. A law on compulsory education was enacted in 1921, and compulsory military service the new year. A language controversy between speakers of Finnish and Swedish festered throughout the 1920s. The unpopular Prohibition Act, enacted in 1919, was repealed in 1932.

The left-wing parties got a taste of power as the country had its first Social Democratic government from 1926 to 1927. The ultra-rightist Lapua Movement, modelled on the Italian Fascist party, staged mass demonstrations in 1929,

demanding a ban on all Communist activity. The enactment of the "Communist laws" of 1930 met this demand. The final effort of the Lapuaists came with an uprising in 1932, but this was put down by the government without bloodshed.

Independent Finland concluded a highly advantageous peace treaty with Soviet Russia in 1920. In the early '20s, Finland pursued cooperation with the "fringe states" Estonia, Latvia, Lithuania and Poland. The League of Nations was the cornerstone of Finnish security policy from the early 1920s to 1935, when the Finns adopted a new, Scandinavian orientation.

▲ The "White General" C.G.E. Mannerheim riding along Helsinki's Esplanade in the victory parade at the end of the Civil War, May 1918. Mannerheim served as regent from December 1918 until K.J. Ståhlberg was sworn in as Finland's first president in the summer of 1919. He was later made marshal and served as commander-in-chief of the Finnish army during the Winter War and Continuation War and then as President of Finland from 1944 to 1946.

The Second World War

Germany and the Soviet Union signed a non-aggression pact in August 1939. In a secret protocol to this pact, Finland was allotted to the Soviet sphere of influence. After the Finns had rejected Soviet territorial demands, the Soviet Union rescinded the 1932 non-aggression pact between the countries, and invaded Finland on November 30, 1939, starting the Winter War. The war ended with the signing of the Treaty of Moscow on March 13, 1940, in which the Soviet Union gained southeastern Finland.

Seeking to boost its security after the Winter War, Finland gradually moved closer to Germany.

▲ The Winter War lasted three and a half months, during which Finland repelled the massive attacks of the Soviet Union time after time. During this exceptionally cold winter, the Soviets learned to fear the Finnish ski patrols, which were likely to turn up without a sound where they were least expected.

▼ The Lotta organization (women's auxiliary corps) provided invaluable services during the war. Its members provisioned and nursed troops even at the front. This photo from the Continuation War shows a nurse giving wounded soldiers water.

When Germany attacked the Soviet Union on 22 June 1941, Finland first declared that it was neutral, but after the Soviets had bombed several Finnish cities, the government drew the conclusion that Finland was in a state of war. This conflict, known as the Continuation War, ended in a truce in September 1944. In addition to the previously ceded territory, Finland had to give up the Petsamo corridor, its only access to the Arctic Ocean. Some 420 000 refugees were moved to Finland from the ceded territory, primarily Karelia.

President of the Republic. He was succeeded in 1946 by J.K. Paasikivi, whose first objective was to establish friendly relations with the Soviet Union. The two countries concluded a Treaty on Friendship, Co-operation and Mutual Assistance in 1948, forming the basis for a policy that became known as the Paasikivi Line.

Over the next few years, Finland's international standing gradually strengthened. The Olympic Games were held in Helsinki in 1952, and that same year the last delivery of Finland's war repara-

The terms of the truce were confirmed in the Treaty of Paris, signed in 1947.

From Paasikivi to Kekkonen

Towards the end of the war, Marshal Mannerheim, commander-in-chief of the Army, was elected

▲ In addition to imposing territorial concessions, the 1947 Treaty of Paris obliged Finland to pay the Soviet Union 300 million dollars' worth of war reparations. The reparations were paid off in the form of industrial goods, mainly metal products. Finland was the only country to pay off its war reparations in full. The last trainload of goods was sent off to the Soviet Union in 1952.

tions to the Soviet Union crossed the border. In 1955 Finland was accepted as a member of the United Nations.

Urho Kekkonen was elected President for the first time in 1956. His aim was to increase Finland's room for manoeuvre in international affairs by pursuing an active policy of neutrality, taking the form of numerous initiatives on the international arena. Throughout Kekkonen's presidency, which lasted until autumn 1981, the ever-darkening shadow of the Soviet Union lay over Finland, giving rise to the term "finlandization", first used abroad, but later in Finland, too.

A new assertiveness

Mauno Koivisto was elected president in 1982. He was succeeded in 1994 by Martti Ahtisaari, the first Finnish head of state to be elected by direct popular vote.

The major upheavals set in motion in the late 1980s, ending the division of Europe and leading to the collapse of the Soviet Union, were reflected in Finland as a freeing of the psychological climate and greater latitude in foreign policy. The nation began to assert itself and take new international initiatives. In 1989 the country finally joined the Council of Europe, and in 1995 it became a member of the European Union.

▼ Finland joined the European Union on 1 January 1995. The Finnish Parliament raised the European flag before daybreak.

SCIENTISTS AND EXPLORERS

Pehr Kalm (1716–1779) was appointed professor of economics at the Academy of Turku in 1747. That same year he set off on a four-year expedition to North America. The multi-volume account of his travels, translated into German, English and Dutch during his lifetime, made him an international celebrity.

Adolf Erik Nordenskiöld (1832–1901) was the father of Finnish mineralogy and an internationally renowned explorer. Having given up an attempt to reach the North Pole, in 1878–79 he became the first man to sail the Northeast Passage, the sea route following the north coast of Eurasia from Norway to the Bering Straits.

Edvard Westermarck (1862–1939) was a world-famous sociologist, who held a professorship in both Finland and Britain. His principal research themes are shown by the titles of two of his chief works, *The History of Human Marriage* (1891) and *The Origin and Development of Morals* (1906–1908). He carried out his most thoroughgoing field studies in Morocco.

A.I. Virtanen (1895–1973) was the father of Finnish biochemistry. He was a professor at the University of Helsinki from 1931 to 1948, when he became a member of the Academy of Finland. In 1945 he was awarded the Nobel Prize for Chemistry for a special fodder conservation method he had developed.

Georg Henrik von Wright (b. 1916) is one of the leading philosophers of the 20th century. He has served as professor at the universities of Helsinki, Cambridge and Cornell, and has been a member of the Academy of Finland since 1961. He has studied deontology, the logic of norms and ethics. Perhaps the best-known of his books is *Explanation and Understanding* (1971).

A CHRONOLOGY OF FINNISH HISTORY

1155 The Swedes' First Crusade to the southwest coast of Finland.
1238 The Swedes' Second Crusade to Häme.
1293 The Swedes' Third Crusade to the end of the Gulf of Finland.
1323 Sweden and Novgorod conclude the Treaty of Pähkinäsaari. The eastern border of Finland is drawn for the first time.
1548 Mikael Agricola translates the New Testament into Finnish.
1550 Founding of Helsinki.
1640 Founding of the Academy of Turku (precursor of the present-day University of Helsinki).
1721 Sweden and Russia conclude the Treaty of Uusikaupunki.
1776 The first newspaper in Finnish is published.
1808 Russian invasion of Finland.

1809 Sweden and Russia conclude the Treaty of Hamina. Russia annexes Finland.

1812 Helsinki becomes the capital of Finland.

1835 The *Kalevala*, the Finnish national epic, is published.

1860 Finland obtains its own currency, the *markka*.

1863 The Language Manifesto. Finnish is to gain equivalent status with Swedish within 20 years.

1863 The Diet begins to convene on a regular basis.

1878 Compulsory military service introduced. Finland obtains its own army.

In 1816, the German architect Carl Ludvig Engel was commissioned by the Tsar to design the centre of Helsinki, the new capital of the Grand Duchy. Engel produced an elegant blend of the Neo-Classical traditions of Berlin and St Petersburg. Senate Square is still flanked, as in the drawing from left to right, by the University, the University Library and St Nicholas' Church (now the Cathedral). Only the guardhouse in front of the church has been demolished and replaced by broad stairs.

1899–1905 First period of "Russification".

1907 Finland obtains a unicameral parliament, the *eduskunta*.

1909–17 Second period of "Russification".

1917 Finland declares independence on December 6.

1918 Civil war breaks out on January 28.

1919 Republican form of government. K.J. Ståhlberg is elected President.

1920 Peace treaty concluded between Finland and Soviet Russia.

1921 Compulsory education enacted.

The 1952 Olympic Games of Helsinki have been called the last genuine sports festival.

1922 Compulsory military service enacted.

1932 Prohibition repealed.

1932 Finland and Soviet Union sign non-aggression pact.

1939 Soviet Union attacks Finland on November 30; Winter War begins.

1940 Winter War ends with the Treaty of Moscow on March 13.

1941–44 Continuation War between Finland and Soviet Union.

1946 J.K. Paasikivi elected President.

1952 Olympic Games in Helsinki.

1956 Urho Kekkonen elected President.

1982 Mauno Koivisto elected President.

1989 Finland becomes member of the Council of Europe.

1994 Martti Ahtisaari elected President.

1995 Finland becomes member of the European Union on January 1.

A Society of Nordic Values

The State

The historical foundation of Finland was the Scandinavian yeoman farmer's society. It is the only republic to have developed on this basis; and yet the Finnish President has a far greater political role than the monarchs of the other Scandinavian countries.

Finland is a democracy with parliamentary representation. Political power is vested in the people and wielded by the Parliament. Parliament is the supreme legislative body comprising 200 members elected for a four-year term. In addition to its role as legislator, Parliament has extensive powers to supervise the Government's actions in preparing decisions taken by the European Union and in formulating Finland's position.

The Finnish Constitution guarantees to all citizens extensive individual rights corresponding to those enumerated in the UN Declaration of Human Rights. The status of the Swedish-speaking minority is guaranteed in the Constitution and in the Language Act, its offshoot: in practice, this status is problem-free. Citizens are free to conduct their official business in either Finnish or Swedish, as they prefer. There has been no tension between the language groups for many decades now.

Integration

Finland joined the European Union as a result of a referendum held in 1994. Finland's accession took place in 1995, simultaneously with that of Sweden and Austria. During the early years of member-

▼ Finland's new government in spring 1999. It is made up of the Social Democrats, the Conservatives, the Swedish People's Party, the Left-Wing Alliance and the Greens. The Agriculture Minister is an independent. Prime Minister Paavo Lipponen is in the centre.

▶ Many farmers today have diversified from traditional agriculture. Thus, many farms run shops offering their own produce and other goods besides. Farm tourism provides a welcome source of additional income.

ship, the decline in the Union's popularity was far less marked in Finland than in the other new Member States. For most Finns, membership implies an unspoken, subconscious sense of greater security, although the Union provides no security guarantees. The most serious problems with adjustment are agricultural. The Common Agricultural Policy (CAP) does not make allowance for the special circumstances of farming in northern latitudes. Finland has had difficulty in adapting its cereals production to the CAP, and farmers' income has decreased significantly.

Finland has 16 members in the European Parliament and three votes in the Council of Ministers. Finland holds the Presidency of the Council during the latter half of 1999. The EU's first Ombudsman is a Finn. Finland entered the third stage of economic and monetary union (EMU) in January 1999, together with the majority of Member States. The Governor of the Bank of Finland was appointed member of the Executive Board of the European Central Bank.

The Grand Committee of Parliament oversees Finnish interests in preparing and implementing EU decisions. The Prime Minister outlines to the Grand Committee matters to be dealt with at European Councils (summit meetings of Union leaders) and reports on the talks to the committee afterwards.

The committee is kept informed about new Union legislation from the beginning of the drafting progress. Ministers appear before the committee to explain the positions adopted by their representatives at preliminary talks. The Grand Committee meets on Fridays, inviting ministers to present their views and hear Parliament's position on issues falling within their remit that are scheduled to be dealt with in the EU Council the following week.

In defence terms, Finland is a non-aligned country, participating in the work of the WEU, the defence arm of the European Union, in the capacity of observer.

The President

The head of state is the President of the Republic, elected by direct popular vote for a six-year term. The President has the power to make decisions on foreign and security policy, to appoint and dismiss ministers and leading civil servants, judges and officers. He/she is also commander-in-chief of the defence forces. The President submits Government bills to Parliament, and ratifies Acts of Parliament and approves decrees on their implementation as well as on administrative matters. Although not directly answerable to Parliament, the President must rely on the support of the Government, which in turn must have Parliament's confidence. In theory the supreme guardian of the administration, in practice the President's decision is always based on the proposal of the competent minister, and only acquires the force of law once ratified by the minister in question.

Leadership of foreign and security policy was for many years the President's most important prerogative. Its constitutional definition remained unchanged for over 70 years, although in practice the President's power varied according to Finland's security policy situation and the political personality of the incumbent.

In the years between the wars, presidents hardly ever asserted their powers in foreign policy. This was partly because Finland steered clear of international crises, but also because the early incumbents were either passive in the foreign policy field or politically weak.

At the time the Winter War (1939–40) broke out, the President was old, ailing and fearful. The real power was in the hands of the three most powerful members of the Government. By 1941, when the Continuation War broke out, a new President was in office. Although he was forceful, active and intelligent, the country's foreign policy was driven by the charismatic and highly popular Marshal C.G.E. Mannerheim, to whom the President had surrendered command of the army.

▼ Martti Ahtisaari was the first Finnish president to be elected by direct popular vote. He regularly travels around the country meeting ordinary Finns.

FINLAND'S PRESIDENTS:

K. J. Ståhlberg	1919–1925
L. Kr. Relander	1925–1931
P. E. Svinhufvud	1931–1937
Kyösti Kallio	1937–1940
Risto Ryti	1940–1944
C. G. E. Mannerheim	1944–1946
J. K. Paasikivi	1946–1956
Urho Kekkonen	1956–1982
Mauno Koivisto	1982–1994
Martti Ahtisaari	1994–

During the Cold War, the fundamental problem of Finnish security policy was how to defend against the ideological and political expansionism of the Soviet Union. The balance between tactical appeasement and strategic self-defence depended at all times on the personal contribution of the President.

During this period the presidents – J.K. Paasikivi followed by Urho Kekkonen – kept an iron grip on Finland's foreign policy, relying on their personal authority. Kekkonen remained in office for 25 years. During this period, his inner circle gradually gained an increasingly powerful role alongside the Government. Its influence was exercised by means of statements issued either directly by the President or by his intermediaries. This arrangement was necessary to reassure the Soviet Union; in it there were also, however, elements of a struggle for domination of domestic policy on the part of the President and his closest associates. This linking up of foreign and domestic policy ended with the Kekkonen era in the early 1980s.

At this time, the locus of power in security matters began to shift to the Government. The transition advanced gradually, with occasional lapses, in the 1980s during the presidency of Mauno Koivisto, but accelerated after he was succeeded by Martti Ahtisaari in the 1990s. When Finland joined the European Union, the Constitution was amended to transfer the responsibility for foreign and security policy decisions to be made within the Union from the President to the Prime Minister, thus bringing them under parliamentary control. Owing to our country's long presidential tradition, this change has been slow to take effect.

Until the early 1990s, the President was elected by a complicated indirect method, the outcome depending on negotiations between the political parties as much as on the popular vote. The direct popular election method adopted in the early '90s was expected to increase presidential power, but in fact this does not seem to have been the case.

The Constitution

The Finnish Constitution has proved exceptionally long-lived. The Constitution Act (*hallitusmuoto*), which lays down the roles and balance of power between the Parliament, Government and President, survived both the Second World War and the Cold War. The national election system and the Parliament Act (*valtiopäiväjärjestys*), on which parliamentary procedure is based, date back to the years before the First World War.

The constitutional democracy functioned virtually without a hitch even during Finland's war against the Soviet Union in the days of the Second World War.

Apart from Britain, Finland was the only country to have taken part in the Second World War in which postwar reconstruction could begin on the basis of a constitution enacted before the war.

The strong constitutional position of the President was initially due to the situation in Finland just after the country became independent in 1917. Following the Civil War of 1918, it was felt that to prevent further unrest, a strong executive was needed. Some of the presidential powers actually derived from the old Constitution adopted in the late 18th century, when Finland was still under Swedish rule. The key constitutional provisions remained in force throughout the period of Russian rule (1809–1917).

For a long time, the President had the right to dissolve Parliament in mid-term, but this right was exercised on only a very few occasions, most recently in the early 1970s. The right of initiative in the dissolution of Parliament was transferred in the early '90s to the Prime Minister. At the same time, the opposition was deprived of the possibility of voting by a qualified minority to shelve a bill until after the next elections. Following the introduction of the normal parliamentary system of majority voting, governments have remained in power throughout the election period despite being based usually on a broad coalition.

A new constitutional reform is now under way. As a result, the parliamentary groups will play a more prominent role in ministerial appointments. The President's power to decide on the appointment of senior civil servants will also probably be curtailed. The President will retain the right to issue decrees, but this power will depend more directly than before on Government approval. The President's leading role in security policy will also be diminished.

▼ **The power belongs to the people. The people's elected delegates electing Finland's first president, K.J. Ståhlberg.**

The constitutional amendments are currently going through a hearing process in Parliament. The new Parliament elected in 1999 can either pass or reject the new Constitution, the contents of which were decided in autumn 1998 as one of the last acts of the outgoing Parliament. The main purpose of the exercise is to consolidate the constitutional provisions included in several different acts into one single act. Most of the amendments introduced are relatively minor, but their overall impact is to strengthen the status of the Prime Minister and thus of Parliament.

In principle, this will slightly reduce the formal powers of the President. The ceremonial and symbolic significance of the presidency, however, is so strong that the President will remain the leading force in the Finnish political system. The influence of the President in the future is likely to depend more on intellectual and moral leadership and media skills than on the formal powers conferred by the Constitution.

The political parties

Finland has had a system of general and equal suffrage since 1906, which is when women received the vote. The voting age is 18. Over one third of all MPs are women. The parliamentary elections are held on a proportional basis, which favours remote, sparsely settled regions and large parties. Nonetheless, new political and non-aligned movements spring up constantly, often playing a major role particularly in local elections.

The three biggest parties dominate the political scene. Following the civil war (fought right after Finland became independent), the Social Democratic Party steered the labour movement in the direction of a Western-type democracy. During the years of uncertainty following the Second World War, the Social Democrats were the mainstay of the struggle against Soviet pressure and the communist bid for power. The Social Democrats are backed financially and ideologically by the powerful labour unions. The Centre Party, which originally represented rural interests, has retained a strong position even though the relative size of the agricultural population has long been no higher than on the Continent. The conservative National Coalition is the third major political force, having developed from a middle-class urban party in the direction of a nationwide white-collar workers' party.

The three main parties are followed by three midsize parties. The Left-Wing Alliance is the heir to the once mighty communist movement. The Greens first appeared on the political scene in the early 1980s, and have gradually consolidated their position, entering the Government for the first time in the late 1990s. The Swedish People's Party defends the interests of the speakers of Finland's minority language; its representation in Parliament is roughly the same as the ratio of Swedish-speakers to the overall population. The party seeks to maintain its influence by participating in every Government.

In addition to those mentioned above, there are generally from two to four smaller parties in Parliament, some of them the last survivors of political movements that are losing momentum, others pioneers of new, rising parties. The system of proportional representation makes it very difficult for these fringe groups to acquire the critical mass needed to consolidate their position among the mid-size parties.

ty's former chairman was implicated. The Conservatives were favoured to win the 1999 elections, and the opposition Centre Party was also expected to do well.

Unemployment had decreased markedly during the past term, and disposable income of households had grown slowly but surely.

▲ Around the turn of the century, many associations advocated general and equal suffrage, which meant that women, too, should have the right to vote. Legislation to this effect was passed in 1906. Here, the constitutive meeting of the Finnish Working Women's Association, 1900.

The parliamentary elections of 1999

The Social Democrats were hard hit towards the end of the 1995–99 parliamentary term by a financial scandal in which the par-

The outcome of the elections was decided by the favourable economic outlook.

The Social Democrats lost 12 seats, but retained their position as the largest party. The Centre Party gains were smaller than expected, as the party platform's call for restricting the power of the trade unions scared off many voters who preferred security to radical change. The Conservative Party chairman won a record number of votes in Helsinki, but the Conservatives still won fewer seats than the Centre Party.

The basic political composi-

DISTRIBUTION OF SEATS IN PARLIAMENT FOLLOWING THE 1999 ELECTIONS

	% der	Sitze
Social Democratic Party (SDP)	22,9	51
Centre Party (KESK)	22,4	48
National Coalition (Conservative Party, KOK)	21,0	46
Left-Wing Alliance (VAS)	10,9	20
Greens	7,3	11
Swedish People's Party (RKP)	5,1	12
Christian League (SKL)	4.2	10
Reform Group (REM)	1,1	1
Basic Finns (PERUS)	1,0	1

tion of the government remained unchanged, but it represented a noticeable shift to the right compared with Lipponen's first government. The enforced restructuring of the government economy had eroded the Social Democrats' zeal for reform. What the Finns expect from their new government is competent administration rather than dramatic reform.

Parliament

Under the Constitution, Parliament is the supreme branch of government. In practice, however, parliamentary legislation and other decision-making tends to be based on Government proposals. The country's general political direction is laid down in the Government programme, drawn up after parliamentary elections when the cabinet is formed. The Government measures the degree of confidence it enjoys in Parliament by submitting its programme for debate in Parliament.

The content of Government bills submitted to Parliament depends largely on the senior civil servants of the various ministries, who draft the legal texts and explanatory memorandums. In theory, Parliament is free to amend these texts as a result of its debates in committee and plenary sessions; the Finnish political tradition, however, is such that Parliament rarely tampers with the substance of Government bills.

In practice, all parliamentary

▼ Riitta Uosukainen,
Speaker of Parliament.

groups included in the government coalition are bound by the decisions agreed on by the ministers concerning texts drafted by the civil service. In recent years, however, the parliamentary groups have shown signs of adopting a more active approach: even MPs of Government parties have proposed Parliament amendments to Government bills, and have pushed them through, too.

Every Government bill is debated four times by the full Parliament. Following a preliminary debate in plenary session, the bill is referred to the appropriate committee. An often quite extensive series of hearings ensues, during which the background and impact of the bill are examined in detail. Committee meetings are closed to the public. Debates in committee often have a real impact on individual posi-

tions, and are only in part tied to political affiliations.

The first reading is based on the report drafted by the committee. The report may suggest several amendments on the wording and details of the bill, but rarely any major change to its essential content.

The second reading usually ends with a vote to adopt the amendments proposed in the committee report as they stand. Individual MPs may here propose further amendments to the text, but it is very rare for such changes to be adopted.

At the third reading, the Parliament either adopts or rejects the text in the wording previously approved. Now an Act of Parliament, the text becomes law once the President has confirmed it. The President has a temporary right of veto. Even if the President exercises this right, however, the next elected Parliament may overrule the President and adopt the Act.

Members of Parliament may also propose for adoption by Parliament a new Act or an amendment to existing provisions. Government bills, however, must be dealt with first. Acts based on MP initiatives are very rarely adopted; recently no more than two or three times per parliamentary term.

A Parliamentary question hour is held weekly, and frequently broadcast live to the nation. Members may make oral questions to the Ministers, who must respond immediately. MPs may also submit written questions to the Government on any matter of their choice. The Minister responsible must provide a written answer within three weeks.

The social partners

The labour and management organizations concluded the first comprehensive collective agreement in the late 1960s, laying down the guidelines for agreements in all the different sectors. In addition to wages and other working conditions, such agreements include provisions on taxation and social policy. Collective bargaining has now settled into a well-established pattern, with the Government playing an increasingly important mediating role in the talks. The "tripartite" agreement reached with this method formally binds only the labour and management organizations involved, but in practice it is final: if Parliament were to enact legislation conflicting with the tripartite agreement, the result would be a serious political crisis. The organizations have therefore gradually taken over some of the power originally vested in Parliament, although a Parliament decision is still required to bring the agreements formally into force.

The powerful negotiating position of the employees' organizations is based on Finland's exceptionally high degree of organized labour: over 80% of the workforce are union members. The pressure for joining a union is strong, as earnings-related unemployment benefits are only paid to members of an unemployment insurance association, the largest of which are run by the unions. The membership fees are deducted by the employer and paid direct to the unions. If more than half the employees in a sector are union members, collective agreements in that sector also cover non-members.

▶ The Finns are more cautious about resorting to industrial action than other nations. This picket's sign reads "Even nurses should be paid".

General political trends

From the early years of independence right up to the Cold War period, Finland's governments tended to be short-lived. It was quite common for talks to begin on the composition and programme of the next government as soon as a new government was sworn in. With economic progress and a more peaceful social climate, governments have become more enduring. From the 1980s, they have stayed in power for the full four-year parliamentary term.

In recent decades, governments have been formed in coalition by two of the three main parties, generally with the support of the Swedish People's Party. The government of Paavo Lipponen, which came into power in the latter half of the 1990s and again in 1999, have the broadest political base seen to date, consisting of the Social Democrats and the conservative National Coalition together with the Left-Wing Alliance, the Swedish People's Party and the Greens. For

the first time in Finnish history, the conservatives and the extreme left thus sit in the same Cabinet; and the Green League also made history by being the first European environmental party to enter a national government.

During the Cold War, the President alone was responsible for defining and implementing the basic lines of foreign and security policy. The President tended to see the Foreign Minister as his personal aide-de-camp. The removal of the Soviet threat and membership of the European Union have led to a normalization of security policy. The foreign policy role of the Prime Minister has strengthened and the *de facto* influence of the President has diminished, although his constitutional powers remain unchanged.

Almost as soon as it had taken office in spring 1995, the Lipponen Government presented Parliament with an extensive report defining a new orientation for Finnish security policy. In it Finland gave up the neutrality guarded so jealously throughout the Cold War as the only viable strategy of defence against Soviet pressure.

The security policy report redefined Finland's international position on the basis of EU mem-

▼ Representatives of the five government parties negotiating the composition of the cabinet, 1995.

bership, military non-alignment and an independent defence. The Parliament debated the report in two sessions, each lasting several days. Previously, the security policy had been determined by the President alone, and during the Cold War no-one had even dared to put it down in writing. Now Parliament debated the policy in public and required an undertaking from Government to present a new proposal to Parliament as soon as there was any need to modify the approved policy.

The Government adopted the same parliamentary procedure in requesting authorization for Finnish troops to participate in UN peacekeeping operations in former Yugoslavia. Two years after the report on security policy, the Government submitted for Parliament approval a basic document on the goals of Finland's defence policy and the structure and function of the Defence Forces.

In 1990, the public debt was only about 10% of gross domestic product. Then recession set in, with soaring unemployment and a bank crisis which rocked the very foundation of the financial system. The public finances were undermined by overly generous unemployment benefits and welfare. Finland had a serious budget

▲ Elisabeth Rehn, the UN Secretary-General's special envoy to Bosnia, talking with refugees.

deficit throughout the early '90s, and the net debt continued to grow even when the economy began to recover in the latter half of the decade. Towards the end of the '90s, the public debt was approximately 70% of GDP.

Even before the recession, Finland had had one of the world's highest tax rates. Now only the Swedes and the Danes pay higher income taxes. Finland's overall tax burden is about 10 percentage points higher than that of Germany; compared with the United States, the difference is 20 percentage points. The national income tax is sharply progressive: the marginal tax in the highest income brackets is over 60%.

Administration

The Government currently consists of the Prime Minister and 17 other ministers. The administration comprises 12 sectoral ministries. Ministers have extensive independent powers to run their ministries and subordinate agencies. The Government bills submitted to Parliament are drafted in the ministries.

Finland is divided administratively into four provinces and 455 municipalities, or local authorities. The latter are required by law to provide welfare services. Their main source of income is from the municipal tax, a standard rate levied on income and collected in conjunction with the progressive State income tax. The State also pays the local authorities to provide welfare services. This sum, known as the 'State share' is calculated in proportion to population and accounts for some 40 per cent of local government income.

The local authorities decide independently on how best to produce the required services with the funds at their disposal. The main services for which they are responsible are health care and hospitals, basic education, social services, fire-fighting and rescue services. They also maintain a library system which covers the whole country and is among the most effective in the world. The local authorities have wide-ranging powers in physical planning. The maintenance of local infrastructure is in part organized along profit-making business principles. This applies to water supply and sewerage and in part to heat and electricity generation and the operation of ports.

The local authorities lay down their own municipal tax rate on the basis of their needs for financing the required services. The rate ranges from 16 to 20 per cent. Political decisions on taxation, finance, administration and town planning are taken by the municipal council. Council elections, based on universal and equal suffrage, are held every four years. In addition to Finnish citizens, foreigners who are permanent residents in the municipality may vote.

The local branches of the main parliamentary parties dominate Finnish local politics, but many councils feature substantial independent groups. A large proportion of MPs are also municipal councillors, and many of them hold leadership positions in local government.

The Åland Islands in the northern Baltic Sea enjoy special status, having been declared a de-

▶ Finnish libraries have kept up with the times by making use of new digital aids. Lending figures for traditional books are still high, nonetheless. In this country of 5.1 million inhabitants, the average Finn borrowed 20 books a year in 1997.

militarized zone by international treaty. Historically, the roots of this status go back to the Crimean War fought in the mid nineteenth century. The islands' international position and autonomy were confirmed in the Åland Self-Government Act. Passed in the 1920s, this act enshrines the linguistic and cultural rights of Åland's Swedish-speaking population. The central government is represented by a Governor appointed by the President of the Republic, but the day-to-day business of government in the islands is handled by the Åland Provincial Assembly, elected by popular vote.

Residents of mainland Finland are not entitled to own land in Åland. The men of Åland are exempted from compulsory military service, instead of which they may opt to serve in the lighthouse and pilot service run by the province's civilian government. Under Finland's Treaty of Accession to the European Union, there is a customs border between Åland and the mainland, and the same rules apply to trade across this border as those which apply to trade between Finland and non-EU countries.

The welfare state

From the 1960s on, Finland has built up a Nordic welfare state, which provides a comprehensive – and expensive – range of services. Welfare services account for approximately one quarter of the State budget, and for over 40 per cent of local government expenditure. Apart from the excellent public hospitals, the largest expenditure item is the extensive system of family support. Parents of new-born children are entitled to almost a full year's parental leave, during which they are paid an allowance determined on the basis of their previous earnings. This leave may be extended until the child reaches the age of three, although the allowance is reduced. All children under school age are entitled to public day-care services. The family allowance, staggered according to the number of children, is one of the largest single expense items in the budget. Compulsory education applies to children between the ages of 7 and 17. The nine-year comprehensive school, including tuition, books and school meals, is free of charge. Those who complete their compulsory education in upper secondary school must pay for certain items, such as books. No tuition fees are charged for vocational or higher education. The State grants an allowance to all students over 17.

Publicly-run health centres and hospitals provide their services virtually free of charge. The sickness insurance system, maintained with tax revenues, covers the cost of almost all prescription drugs. Unemployment benefits are earnings-related and represent 50–60% of the beneficiary's previous wages, more than this for families with children. Pensions, fully vested after 40 years of service, amount to between 60% and 66% of wages. All those over 65 are also entitled to a basic national pension.

During the early 1990s, budget retrenchment led to significant reductions in welfare benefits. The local authorities had to go on providing statutory services with reduced State funding. Earnings-related benefits were cut and eligibility rules were tightened, and family allowances were reduced somewhat, but the basic policy of maintaining the Nordic welfare state remained unchanged. Even after the cuts made during the recession, social security remained more or less at the level attained in the late 1980s.

Finland's health care and family policy are financed with taxes, while the costs of pensions and earnings-related unemployment benefits are divided between employees, employers and State, the State's contribution being the largest and the employees' the smallest.

The Courts

In accordance with the classic doctrine of the separation of powers, the Finnish judiciary is independent of the legislative and executive branches of government. Its only connection with the executive is that the President appoints the justices of the high courts. Thereafter they, like all other judges, are virtually undismissible. The court system is three-tiered. Only cases having the nature of a precedent or in which an obvious procedural error has been committed go all the way to the highest level. The constitution of ad hoc courts is forbidden. The prosecuting authority, headed by the State Prosecutor's Office, is independent of both the courts and the police.

In addition to the general courts, there are several specialized courts dealing, among other matters, with housing, insurance, water and market affairs. Administrative courts act as courts of appeal in matters of administrative procedure. Charges brought against a minister or one of the country's chief law officers are examined by the High Court of Impeachment. The decision to impeach a minister is made by Parliament, but the conditions to be met are so stringent that impeachment on political grounds is not possible. The Court of Impeachment has been convened only on a handful of occasions.

The Chancellor of Justice is the supreme guardian of legality. He/she attends all Government meetings and may intervene if there is a danger that the form or legal content of a decision may conflict with the law. Any citizen whose rights have been violated may submit a complaint to the Chancellor of Justice about the actions of the authorities. The Parliamentary Ombudsman supervises the legality of official actions and examines complaints by citizens; he/she is also responsible for monitoring the prison system and the defence forces.

Defence

The national defence is based on a system of regional defence networks covering the whole country. It is founded on the principle of compulsory military service for

men. Every year, an age group of approximately 30 000 Finns is trained. This figure usually includes about 500 women, for whom military service is voluntary. The service period for conscripts trained for command posts is approximately one year, that for the rank and file six months.

The task of the training units is to produce manpower for the wartime army, in which each reservist has a specific task. The reserve troops are frequently called up for refresher courses, attended by 35,000 persons every year. The trained reserve forces are about half a million strong, or almost 10% of the entire population, which is the highest ratio of trained reservists in Europe.

Finland is prepared to mobilize 22 brigades armed for regional defence and three rapid deployment units armed for effective, mobile defence aimed at the point of main effort. The wartime strength of the

▼ The fighter aircraft used by the Finnish Air Force are the US Hornet and the UK Hawk.

▲ Harri Holkeri, former Prime Minister of Finland, has acted as Independent Chairman of the Northern Ireland Talks Process. Here, Holkeri holding up the Shamrock Award.

defence forces is 430,000 soldiers.

The Finnish Air Force is currently replacing its air fleet: its main aircraft as of the year 2000 will be the American F-18 (Hornet) and the British Hawk. The armoured vehicles of the land forces were originally purchased from the former Soviet Union and GDR, but retrofitted with Finnish signalling and fire control technology. The backbone of the coastal defence consists of Swedish-made marine target missiles based on fast battleships and land-based mobile launchpads, a highly developed sonar system and an effective mine system.

The concept of compulsory military service is widely backed by popular opinion. Opinion polls indicate that even during the Cold War, when Finland had an agreement with the Soviet Union containing provisions on military co-

operation, well over two thirds of the respondents were prepared to take up arms to defend their country in any contingency. During the 1990s this readiness to defend the country and the belief in Finland's defensive capability have increased markedly.

Finland is involved in the NATO Partnership for Peace programme and the Euro-Atlantic Partnership Council. Finnish peacekeeping troops are currently engaged in UN missions in Lebanon and Macedonia. A Finnish light infantry battalion is taking part in the SFOR operation in Bosnia under NATO command.

Although Finland's security policy is based on military neutrality, the Finns do not rule out the possibility of entering into an alliance. They generally have strong reservations about NATO membership, however, which shows that for the first time in centuries the Finns feel secure even in the military sense of the word.

The Church

The Catholic Church extended its hold over most of Finland in the 12th century, when the Swedes conquered western Finland, Christianizing it in the process. Meanwhile, the Principality of Novgorod was busy propagating the Orthodox creed in Karelia and eastern Finland. The Lutheran doctrine of Reformation took over from the Catholic Church during the 16th century, since which Finland and the other Nordic countries have been the foremost stronghold of Lutheranism in the world.

In principle, the Finnish State is neutral in religious matters, but the Evangelical-Lutheran Church is mentioned in the Constitution Act, and its administration and activities, as well as those of the Finnish Orthodox Church, are regulated by the Church Act, issued by Parliament. Both Churches have extensive autonomy, and their funding is secured by the right to levy a tax on their members. This in fact provides most of their income. Parishes keep population registers and are responsible for the upkeep of church buildings of cultural and historical value and of graveyards. When a new Parliament convenes, the opening ceremony always includes an Evangelical-Lutheran service.

The role of the Lutheran Church as the principal national church is shown by the fact that the Evangelical-Lutheran congregations had 4,400,000 members in 1997, or 85.6% of the population. Several large and influential revivalist movements operate within the Church. They were established in the nineteenth century by charismatic lay preachers and priests. The archbishop's see is Turku. There are eight dioceses; all of the country's Swedish-speaking congregations belong to the diocese of Borgå (Porvoo).

Finland's second largest religious community is the Orthodox Church, which has 54,000 members, or 1.1% of the population. The church is under the direct protection of the patriarchate of Constantinople. The archbishop's see is Kuopio, and there are three dioceses: Helsinki, Karelia and Oulu.

The Pentecostal revival movement numbers some 50,000 baptized members plus a considerable number of their children. Jehovah's Witnesses have 17,000 members in Finland, the Free Church of Finland has 13,000, the Catholic Church 6,000 and the Jewish congregations 1,100 members. The number of Muslims has increased more than tenfold over the last ten years, but only a handful – fewer than one thousand – are registered as members of official religious communities.

Over 634,000 Finns, or 12.3% of the population, are classified as non-denominational. During the 1990s, the number of people leaving the Church has slightly exceeded those joining it. There are few atheists, however, as half of those who are not members of a church consider themselves to be

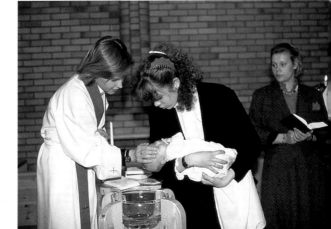

▶ The first Finnish women priests were ordained in 1988; there are no women bishops yet.

Christians, and only 16% count themselves atheists.

The supreme decision-making body of the Evangelical-Lutheran Church is the Synod, which makes proposals on amendments to the Church Act and approves the statutes of the Church. It also discusses questions of doctrine and creed and approves the Church's service books.

The Evangelical-Lutheran Church comprises 587 parishes (1999), which have considerable financial and operational independence. The parishes are served by some 1,800 clergy, over one fifth of whom are women. The first women priests were ordained in 1988. The Church and parishes employ some 19,000 people all told (1997). The diversity of jobs available is shown by the fact that among those employed by the parishes were 803 church musicians, 1147 social workers, 1207 youth workers and 2464 child care workers.

The work of the parishes affects virtually the whole population in one way or another. Finns of all age groups attend major church ceremonies, which include baptism, confirmation, marriage and burial. 89% of the new-born are baptized, and 97% of funerals are ecclesiastical. Year after year, over 90% of the country's 15-year-olds attend confirmation classes. These usually take the form of a camp lasting over a week, supplemented before or after by a presentation of the parish and by group activities.

The educational and social work done by the parishes, much of it on a voluntary basis, is of major social significance. In its social work, the Church focuses on helping the aged, disabled, alcoholics and drug addicts, and families in financial difficulties. The parishes also run dozens of family counselling centres, and have set up pioneering debt counselling services, self-help activities for the unemployed and "neighbourly help" programmes. Missionary work also has a strong following among the faithful.

The average member of the Church attends divine service twice a year. Although the Finns are thus rather infrequent church-goers, polls indicate that almost half the population (well over half of the women and one third of the men) consider themselves believers. This proportion is highest among the oldest age groups. The majority of those who go to church only a few times a year, and even one fifth of those who never do, think of themselves as believers. Two out of five Finns say that they pray weekly, and half the population at least once a month.

The Economy

The Finnish economy has gone through two complete metamorphoses during the past few decades. First, this once predominantly agrarian country saw the swiftest process of industrialization and urbanization of any country in Europe. More recently, the production of high technology has proliferated, while the traditional smokestack industries have been subjected to wholesale rationalization and internationalization. In many cases, this has led to drastic changes in ownership arrangements. Economic policy became increasingly liberal as Finland struggled to overcome the depression that hit the country in the early 1990s.

These rapid transformations have naturally left their mark on Finnish society. Despite heavy unemployment, however, the country has remained remarkably stable. To be sure, the country will still need time and flexibility to adjust fully to structural changes.

Electronics to the fore

Growth has been fastest in the 1990s in the electronics industry. Finland's flagship company in the field is Nokia, although there are also a number of smaller, more specialized electronics firms. The more conventional electrotechnical industry is represented by the world's third largest lift manufacturer Kone and its offshoot KCI-Konecranes, and by ABB Strömberg, founded over a century ago by a Finnish pioneer of electrical engineering. The sector has been

▶ Jorma Ollila, managing director, has every reason to be proud of his company. Nokia is one of the world's leading manufacturers of mobile phones and a linchpin of the Finnish economy.

FINLAND'S LARGEST INDUSTRIAL AND COMMERCIAL ENTERPRISES IN 1998

Name	Line of business	Turnover FIM billion	billion euros
1. Nokia	Electronics	79	13
2. Stora Enso	Forest industry	62	10
3. Fortum	Energy, oil	51	9
4. UPM-Kymmene	Forest industry	50	8
5. Kesko	Retail chain	36	6
6. Metsäliitto	Forest industry	29	5
7. Tamro	Wholesalers	18	3
8. Outokumpu	Metallurgy	17	3
9. Metra	Machinery	15	3
10. Rautaruukki	Metallurgy	15	3

Source: *Talouselämä* 21/1997

highly regarded in Finland ever since 1887, when young Gottfried Strömberg was appointed lecturer in electrical engineering at the institution today known as the Helsinki University of Technology (cf. the chapter *Scientific feats*).

Of course Finland does not have natural features that particularly favour the growth of the electrical industry – if, indeed, any country has such features. A possible advantage, however, is the fact that the sector does not depend heavily on raw materials.

Nokia, one of Finland's industrial giants since the 1860s, began to take an interest in electronics in the 1960s as an offshoot of its cable manufacturing operations. In the 1970s the company took over the industrial operations of the national telecommunications administration. In the 1980s the group began to specialize, buying up several electronics firms in Sweden, Germany and elsewhere.

There was a period when the company found itself treading water, and had to sell out its computer production to ICL (which still makes computers in Finland). The real breakthrough came in the 1990s, when cellular communications became big business. Nokia has continually streamlined its mobile phone technology, and is now one of the world leaders in the field. Meanwhile, the company has divested itself of many sidelines.

Previously owned by Finnish commercial banks and other institutions, Nokia (like many other major Finnish companies) now has increasingly international ownership arrangements. The lift maker Kone, however, is still controlled by the Herlin family. Its new top-of-the-line product is a

▲ Kone is the world's third biggest manufacturer of lifts and escalators. The company is now marketing its innovative lift without a machine room, which is likely to lead to new applications for elevator technology.

lift without an engine room. Strömberg, now a subsidiary of ABB (Asea Brown Boveri), has concentrated successfully on manufacturing heavy electrical machinery.

Specialized metal products

The metal products sector, which includes both electrical equipment and electronics, is Finland's leading export industry today in terms of both volume of production and jobs.

It is a byword in the business that the Finns are good at making anything "bigger than a horse". We have little chance of competing with standardized products, such as domestic appliances, which re-

quire large production volumes. On the other hand, Finland can be successful in making sophisticated specialized technology, such as state-of-the-art electronics and large-scale industrial systems. A high-tech approach also underlies the very successful Oras water tap.

Not surprisingly, Finland is a leading manufacturer of machin-

▲ Oras taps control water temperature with the push of a button.

ery for the timber and wood-processing industries. Expertise in paper machines is today concentrated in the hands of Valmet, originally set up as the national arms factory. Other machinery for the sector is made by Ahlström, still a family business, and Metso (composed of parts of Valmet and Rauma). Sisu, a maker of heavy lorries and forest tractors, is now a subsidiary of the Partek group, formerly a construction company.

The worldwide shipyard crisis has affected Finland, too, but Kvaerner Masa-Yards, (which has for ten years been in Norwegian ownership) has had considerable success in building luxury cruisers. However, the company is currently looking for a new owner. Icebreakers, Finland's traditional forte, are still going strong. Wärtsilä, a subsidiary of Metra, is now a leading manufacturer of diesel engines for ships and power plants. Another major engineering firm is Tamrock, which makes mining equipment and other heavy machinery.

The metallurgical industry has had to adjust, as domestic mining operations have petered off in the past few years. The Outokumpu company has therefore acquired copper plants and other metal works and mine holdings around the world. The flash smelting method, developed by Outokumpu, is a major Finnish industrial invention. Rautaruukki is a successful steel company.

Living on forests

Finland has traditionally "lived on her forests". The paper industry is still a vital source of exports. Finland is also a major global player in the sawmill and board sector and other mechanical wood-processing industries. The forest industry needs little imported input, which boosts Finland's balance of payments.

The modern wood-processing industry is based on highly automated processes. For a paper machine one hundred metres long, you will only find a handful of employees stationed at computer screens. The need for enormous in-

vestments has led to intense concentration in the sector. There are now three major Finnish wood-processing consortia: the private company UPM-Kymmene, the partly State-controlled, Finnish-Swedish owned Stora Enso, and Metsä-Serla, which is controlled by private forest owners.

There are still numerous small sawmills, but automation and higher value added are buzzwords even in mechanical wood-processing these days.

The wood-processing industry has boosted its ecological impact radically since the 1970s. The modern pulp mill is virtually a closed circuit; its process water is cleaned up and recycled, while waste is incinerated, making the mill self-sufficient in terms of energy. The production of mechanical pulp (groundwood) for newsprint and other paper, however, still requires a great deal of electricity. Finland meticulously recycles its waste paper.

Forests owned by farmers

Finland's vast forests are primarily (54%) in private ownership. The owners are farmers or, increasingly, their citified descendants. Hundreds of thousands of Finns are forest owners. About one third of all forests (mainly in northern Finland) belong to the government, while the wood-processing companies own less than 10%. The situation differs radically from that in other countries. This fragmentation causes some problems with felling; on the other hand, the owners naturally take good care of their inherited woodlands, some of which have been in the family for centuries.

The volume of forest growth has exceeded the volume felled in Finland since the 1960s. Thus there is probably more wood in

◀ The pano-
rama windows
of the Timber-
jack harvester
make it easy for
the operator to
keep an eye on
his progress.

the Finnish forests than ever before. The authorities see to it that reforestation begins immediately after a stand of trees is felled. Trees reach full harvesting size in about 70 years – a great deal faster in the southern parts of the country than in Lapland. Large-scale clear cutting is prohibited.

Forestry methods are much debated in Finland. A powerful harvester may not be a beautiful sight, but who would be prepared these days to set off into the forest with a saw and an axe and to drag the logs through deep snow to the nearest river, as 300 000 men still did back in the 1950s? Today there are only a few thousand lumberjacks left. If it had not been for the rational use of forests, there never would have been a Finnish nation.

Chemicals and energy

The basic chemicals industry in Finland is largely in the hands of two companies originally set up by the government. Kemira's main products include fertilizers and paints, while Neste (now part of Fortum) refines oil and distributes natural gas. Plastic products are made by Uponor, a subsidiary of the Asko Group.

The Finnish building materials industry has dwindled during the 1990s. Joint Nordic arrangements have been concluded for the cement sector. Construction proper suffered severely during the depression, but is now well on the way to recovery.

Electricity has been generated by the State-run Imatran Voima company, industrial energy firms and municipally-owned power plants. Deregulation has brought turmoil to the sector: Finnish and Swedish energy conglomerates have bought up small local power companies, and the latest move was the merger of Imatran Voima and Neste, creating a new energy giant called Fortum.

Despite its 200 000 lakes, Finland is a low-lying country, and hydroelectric power is at a premium. Nonetheless, the Finns have decided to refrain from harnessing their last free-flowing rapids. On the other hand, Finland is a leader in the production of highly

KEY ECONOMIC STATISTICS
(mainly 1996 to 1998)

HOUSING
- total number of homes — 2.4 million
- average size — 76 sq. m.
- space per person — 34 sq.m.
- owner-occupied — 61%

ENERGY SOURCES
- oil — 27%
- papermaking processes etc. — 19%
- nuclear — 17%
- coal — 15%
- natural gas — 9%
- hydroelectric — 9%
- peat — 3%
- imported energy — 2%

Total energy consumption: 32 million toe (tonnes oil equivalent)

ECONOMY (1998)
- gross domestic product — FIM 676 billion (114 billion euros)
- taxes — 47%
- per capita income — FIM 99.100 (16,667 euros)
- unemployment rate — 11%
- net foreign debt — FIM 275 billion (46 billion euros)
- government budget — FIM 191 billion (32 billion euros)
- inflation rate — 1%

TRANSPORT
- private cars — 1.9 million
- roads — 77,782 km
- railway tracks — 5,865 km
- airline passengers — 11.8 million
- telephones — 2.8 million
- mobile telephones — 2.1 million
(1998, the figure rises rapidly)

AGRICULTURE
- number of farms (over 5 ha) — 106.853
- average size of fields — 16 hectares
- yield per hectare (wheat) — 3.7 tonnes
- self-sufficiency rate (cereals) — 74% of consumption
- head of livestock — 1.1 million

FORESTRY
- farmed forest — 26.3 million hectares

- ownership:
  - private — 54%
  - government — 33%
  - companies — 8%
  - other — 5%

- tree species (by volume):
  - pine — 46%
  - spruce — 37%
  - deciduous species — 18%

- annual growth of trees: 75 million cubic metres; commercial felling: 45 million cubic metres (considerable annual fluctuation)

INDUSTRY

	Jobs	Value added billion	
		FIM	euros
Metal products	153,519	46	7.7
Food	42,138	12	2.0
Paper	38,306	19	3.2
Chemicals	34,830	14	2.4
Graphic industry	28,566	8	1.3
Mechanical wood-working	24,770	5	0.8
Power plants etc.	19,231	13	2.2
Metallurgy	16,914	6	1.0
Textiles	16,635	3	0.5
Ceramics	12,175	3	0.5
Furniture	9,076	2	0.3
Mines	3,546	1	0.2
Total	403,531	134	22.5

Workforce
- services — 65%
- industry — 22%
- agriculture — 7%
- construction — 6%

Total — 2.5 million people

efficient back-pressure power and district heating. Nuclear energy, a subject of much debate, covers 15% of the country's overall energy requirement. The other main source of energy is coal, the environmental impact of which is also controversial. Increasing use is being made of natural gas imported from Russia. The peat won from Finland's extensive wetlands is also used locally for power generation.

Food and design

The basic foodstuffs industry was protected by high tariffs until Finland joined the European Union in 1995, opening the floodgates for full-scale competition. The result was a major restructuring of the domestic food-processing sector, although it remained basically in the hands of Finnish farmers. The company Raisio has gained an international reputation with its food fat called Benecol, which reduces blood cholesterol levels.

The Finnish food-processing industry is now busily establishing Nordic and Baltic partnerships. Some of the leading companies in the field are Fazer (confectionery), Paulig (coffee), Hartwall and Sinebrychoff (breweries) and Valio (dairy products). A Finnish company that has gone multinational is the Huhtamäki Group, which manufactures Polarcup packaging.

The leading Finnish pharmaceuticals firm Orion focuses on markets in the neighbouring countries, but has also developed a number of internationally successful trademark drugs. Leiras, a Finnish company that is now a subsidiary of Schering, is one of the world's leading producers of contraceptives.

The consumer goods industry in general has been strongly affected by growing international competition. Mass-produced goods are imported from countries with low production costs, while Finnish companies focus on specialized quality products. Clothes firms include Luhta (L-Fashion) and Marimekko.

The Hackman company is responsible for most of the production known generically as Finnish Design (Arabia porcelain and Iittala glassware, cf. the chapter on design). There are two large furniture manufactur-

▼ In these days of cheap imports, the Finnish textile industry must focus on quality to retain its market shares. In particular, sales of sportswear and other leisurewear are on the rise.

▶ New department stores, supermarkets and shopping malls are springing up constantly in towns and suburbs.

ers (Asko-Sotka and Isku) and several smaller ones. One of these is Artek, which sells furniture designed by Alvar Aalto.

Services

Until quite recently, Finland was essentially an agrarian country with a relatively undeveloped service sector. The rapid increase in earnings and tax rates over the last few decades has largely turned Finland into a self-service country. Moreover, many national and municipal services have been cut during the past few years.

The perishables market was long divided between four retail chains, but this situation has changed completely in the 1990s. The market is dominated by Kesko (K stores), owned by individual retailers, whereas the wholesalers' chain (T stores) has split up. The cooperatives (S stores) surmounted the crisis, whereas the E chain, run by the labour movement, is still in the process of restructuring.

All these changes were dictated by the trend towards ever larger supermarkets and hypermarkets. The largest department store, Stockmann, has survived.

Tourism, hard hit by the depression in the early 1990s, is now well on the way to recovery. Indeed, after a hiatus of 80 years, Finland is now seeing a spate of Russian tourists. The Finns themselves are spending increasing amounts of money on restaurants and tourist attractions such as the ski resorts of Lapland.

The State monopoly on the dis-

▲ All year round, ferries transport passengers and cars to Stockholm, Tallinn and Lübeck and offer cruises on the Baltic Sea.

tribution of alcoholic beverages is now crumbling. For the time being, however, wine and spirits can only be purchased in the State-owned Alko shops. In terms of product range, Alko is well prepared for competition. Most of the price on its products, however, consists of tax.

Half an island

Finland's salient characteristics from the transport point of view are its large size and low population density. With respect to the world outside, it is more than half an island.

Most of the country's imports and exports are transported by sea (the routes are kept open in winter by icebreakers), although nowadays there is also a great deal of transit trade by road with Russia. Within the country, goods are transported mainly by road, while the railways specialize in heavy transports. Inland water transport routes extend from the eastern Gulf of Finland via the Saimaa canal as far as Lake Päijänne in central Finland.

Foreign travellers usually arrive in Finland by air or by sea, although the country is of course connected by road to Russia and to northern Sweden and Norway. The ferries plying the Baltic Sea (Silja Line and Viking Line) are really floating hotels, frequented as much for pleasure and amusement as for getting from one country to another.

Domestic air transport is well-developed. The railways have invested in state-of-the-art rolling stock, and now focus on running a few main lines and Helsinki's commuter traffic. The coach network is extensive, although many rural routes have been suppressed. The main towns are well served by public transport, but in rural areas a car is almost a must. The whole population could easily be seated in the country's two million cars. This is indeed what tends to happen at midsummer, when just about everyone leaves town for a weekend in the country.

Concentration in banking and insurance

The Finnish banking sector was deregulated in the 1980s. This emboldened the savings banks, in particular, to take such excessive risks that by the early 1990s the country found itself with a serious banking crisis on its hands. The government came to the rescue, leaving the taxpayers to foot a bill of at least FIM 40 billion (nearly USD 10 billion); the final sum will not be known until all the real estate and other security taken over by the government has been sold.

Following the bank crisis, most of the savings banks were carved up and shared out between the remaining banks. Under increasing pressure from competition, the two leading commercial banks Kansallis and the Union Bank of Finland merged in 1995 to form Merita Bank. In 1997 Merita merged with Nordbanken of Sweden. The State-owned Posti-pankki (now Leonia) has also been restructured. The only remaining representative of local banking is the cooperative OKO Group. International banks, particularly Scandinavian ones, have rapidly expanded their operations in Finland.

Finnish banking is highly advanced technically. Wages and salaries, for example, have long been paid direct to bank accounts. Automated teller machines are everywhere, and many families pay their bills via home computer. The office network is still shrinking as a result of increasing automation.

The insurance sector is now concentrated in the hands of three companies (Pohjola, Sampo and Tapiola). The extensive branch of the business that handles compulsory pension insurance is largely run by private companies. There has been much discussion of the intertwining of insurance and banking operations, which could lead to the establishment of 'all-purpose financial institutions'.

Banks and insurance companies have long played a key role in Finnish industry, but recently the ties have loosened. Many industries now raise funds via direct worldwide share issues; consequently, the financial institutions' hold on Finnish industry is slipping. Meanwhile, the Helsinki Stock Exchange's turnover has soared during the last twenty years. Hundreds of thousands of Finns now own shares in companies.

◀ The majority of Finns pay their bills and handle most of their other banking transactions via automatic teller or personal computer.

The world's northernmost farming country

Until the 1950s, agriculture was Finland's principal source of livelihood. As a result of successive land reforms, farms were small. Farmers supplemented their income by selling timber and doing forestry work. The number of farms has since declined to one third, or approximately 100,000. Meanwhile the average farm size has risen to about 15 hectares. This trend is bound to continue – not least because Finnish agriculture, formerly fully protected, has been compelled by EU membership to open the doors to competition from imported goods.

Finland is the world's northernmost country in which arable farming is practicable (even in Sweden nearly all the fields are farther south). In the severe climate, crops are small by continental standards, and barely reach maturity just before the first night frosts arrive. Nonetheless, the Finns consider maintaining their own agricultural production a political necessity. Finland's treaty on accession to the European Union therefore allows the country to pay its farmers additional subsidies over and above the general EU support.

Only some 8% of the population now live from agriculture and forestry, and many supplement their income with ancillary occupations. Seeking new sources of income, some farmers have even started raising ostriches, which cope with the cold surprisingly well.

Although the Finns eat a fair amount of fish, fishing is not a major source of livelihood. There are many sports fishermen, however; in winter, one sometimes sees hundreds of 'ice anglers' try-

▼ Animal husbandry is better suited to the climate than arable farming, although good barns are a must to provide shelter in the winter.

ing their luck in the frozen lakes or coastal sea waters. The most important commercial catch is Baltic herring, while the main species fished for sport are perch and pike. Rainbow trout is being farmed in growing quantities – giving rise to criticism on account of the resulting water pollution.

There are more than 200,000 reindeer in Lapland, although actually the 50,000 elk hunted yearly yield more meat. Hunting is the hobby of some 300,000 Finns. Fur farming, on the other hand, is an important though controversial source of livelihood in many rural villages.

Changing ownership structures

Finnish firms were previously owned by either families or institutions. Foreign ownership was restricted significantly until the 1990s. Some 20% of all industry was State-controlled. This was primarily in basic production, which tended to require larger capital investments than Finland's small private sector was able to provide.

Many State-owned companies have been at least partially privatized in recent years. Many of the agency-type State institutions (such as the postal service and railways) have been transformed into commercial enterprises, and efforts have also been made to stimulate competition in other areas. A number of cartels formed by private companies have been broken up.

Since the laws were amended, foreign investors have bought a large number of shares in Finnish companies. Certain firms have joined major groups of companies, particularly joint Nordic ones. On the other hand, since the 1980s Finnish firms have been purchasing many factories, even entire companies, abroad. In some cases, they have paid dear for such boldness; on the other hand, many hold that in narrowly specialized fields the only road to success is to attain international stature.

Foreign investors have tended to adopt a rather passive role in Finland up to now, and the advent of foreign capital is generally seen as a favourable trend. It is likely, however, that the investors expect their capital to be put to more effective use than has been customary in Finland. This used to be due in part to taxation, which tended to favour investments, however dubious they might be. Now the emphasis is generally on profitability and soundness rather than rapid expansion.

Consensus with the trade unions

The key word in Finnish economic policy has been 'consensus', meaning the tendency to seek a common understanding between businesses, trade unions, the national government and other interested parties. Consensus is no bed of roses, however, for agreements are generally preceded by lengthy negotiations, and strikes are not unusual. Generally, however, a compromise can be reached. In this system, abrupt Thatcherite reforms would be impossible; and yet, equilibrium has its value in a small country.

Some of the most important employers' organizations are *Teol-*

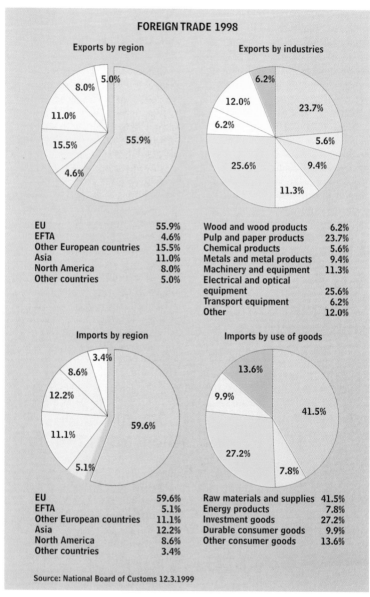

FOREIGN TRADE 1998

Exports by region

EU   55.9%
EFTA   4.6%
Other European countries   15.5%
Asia   11.0%
North America   8.0%
Other countries   5.0%

Exports by industries

Wood and wood products   6.2%
Pulp and paper products   23.7%
Chemical products   5.6%
Metals and metal products   9.4%
Machinery and equipment   11.3%
Electrical and optical
equipment   25.6%
Transport equipment   6.2%
Other   12.0%

Imports by region

EU   59.6%
EFTA   5.1%
Other European countries   11.1%
Asia   12.2%
North America   8.6%
Other countries   3.4%

Imports by use of goods

Raw materials and supplies 41.5%
Energy products   7.8%
Investment goods   27.2%
Durable consumer goods   9.9%
Other consumer goods   13.6%

Source: National Board of Customs 12.3.1999

lisuus ja Työnantajat (Finnish Industry and Employers, TT), *Palvelutyönantajat* (Finnish Service Employers, PT), the Central Chamber of Commerce and the regional chambers of commerce, and the Finnish Confederation of Private Entrepreneurs, which represents small businesses. The various sectors of industry naturally each have their own organization, the most influential of which is the *Maataloustuottajain Keskusliitto* (Central Union of Agricultural Producers, MTK).

The trade unions have three

different central organizations. The largest of these is the *Suomen Ammattiliittojen Keskusjärjestö* (Central Organization of Finnish Trade Unions, SAK), which comprises blue-collar workers and various junior officials and civil servants. The members of the *Suomen Teknisten Toimihenkilöjärjestöjen Keskusliitto* (Confederation of Technical Employee Organizations in Finland) are white-collar workers (including nurses), while *Akava* (Confederation of Unions for Academic Professionals) has as its members holders of academic degrees, from teachers to physicians. At 85%, the Finnish workforce's degree of organization is among the highest in the world.

Recovering from recession

Finnish economic policy has changed radically over the years. True, Finland has engaged in free trade with other West European countries since the 1950s, but the Finnish economy was highly regulated and protectionist in many ways until the mid 1980s. Corporate cooperation and bank-run finance groups were important; some spoke of the promised land of cartels, although the Finns hardly invented these.

We have already mentioned that the money market was liberalized rapidly during the 1980s, leading to a bank crisis. Many companies resorted indiscriminately to loans de-

---

FINNISH BUSINESS LEADERS

Krister Ahlström (b. 1940), leading businessman in a company that still bears the family name

Casimir Ehrnrooth (b. 1931), now somewhat inconspicuous, but still the wire-puller of a powerful business family

Aatos Erkko (b. 1932), leading publisher and perhaps Finland's richest man, but something of an enigma

Matti Honkala (b. 1945), recently appointed general director of Kesko, Finland's largest retail chain

Jukka Härmälä (b. 1945), managing director of the State-owned Enso company

Jere Lahti (b. 1943), general director of SOK (Finnish Co-operative Wholesale Society), a heavyweight in the coop sector

Jouko K. Leskinen (b. 1943), general director of Sampo insurance company, talented insurance strategist

Juha Niemelä (b. 1946), new managing director of UPM-Kymmene

Jorma Ollila (b. 1950), managing director of Nokia and architect of the company's meteoric rise

Christoffer Taxell (b. 1948), general director of Partek, holds the purse-strings of Finland-Swedish capital

Vesa Vainio (b. 1942), general director of Merita Bank, leading banker

Viinanen, Iiro (b. 1944), former owner of a family company and politician, now general director of Pohjola Insurance Group

Matti Vuoria (b. 1951), chairman of the board of Fortum, the new State-owned energy conglomerate

nominated in foreign currency. The collapse of the Soviet Union in the early 1990s did away with virtually all of Finland's government-led, bilateral 'eastern trade'. Since then, however, trade with Russia has revived – now on a private basis.

When the economy overheated in the 1980s, domestic prices soared and Finland lost some of its markets in the west. Domestic and foreign problems combined to send Finland into a deep recession in the early 1990s. At the worst time, over half a million people (about 20% of the population) were unemployed. The country has succeeded in keeping its jobless population housed and fed – indeed, according to some critics so well as to discourage the unemployed from seeking new jobs or occupations. To be sure, some people (such as small entrepreneurs who went bankrupt) genuinely had serious difficulties.

Efforts to correct the situation began in 1992–93, when the Finnish mark was allowed to float. The exchange rate fell by as much as 25%, although it has risen somewhat since. This naturally caused serious losses for those who had taken out currency loans, but exports began to increase again. The social consequences were mitigated by heavy borrowing abroad, which the country could still (fortunately) afford at the time.

Export growth enabled Finland to reattain the 1990 peak level of domestic product by 1995, and GDP has continued to grow since then (by almost 6% in 1997). The unemployment rate, however, has been slow to decrease, as companies have pursued rationalization. In 1999, the unemployment rate may come down to just under 10 per cent, but this does not include the many people who either attend training organized by the government or hold subsidized jobs.

Public sector employment also had to be cut in order to reduce government borrowing and bring taxation down a peg or two. Finland's balance of trade has been in the black since 1992, but government debt and servicing costs are still increasing. Nonetheless, Finland met all the criteria for ecomomic and monetary union in 1998, and adopted the euro among the first countries to do so.

Despite all the difficulties, the country's economic institutions have stood up well to the test. The labour market has concluded wide-ranging, moderate collective agreements, and there have been no major strikes for many years. The trump cards of the Finnish economy in the future will be a high standard of education, general respect of agreements, a low level of corruption and good internal security.

Scientific
Feats

For many years, Finland has been either first, second or third in the world in terms of using cellular phones, the Internet and personal computers. All through the twentieth century, while almost all other European countries have had a government monopoly on communication, Finland has had numerous private telephone companies.

Finland is also one of the world's three major producers of cellular phones. Many of the large cruise ships sailing the high seas were built in Finland. Leading newspapers and magazines around the world are printed on paper that has been made either in Finland or with Finnish-made paper machines.

Present-day Finland is thus very much a high-tech country. Finland is also a European pioneer in information technology and liberalized telecommunication services.

From farms to factories

In 1930, about 60 per cent of the population earned their living as farmers. When World War II ended in 1945, Finland was still a relatively poor agricultural country – and farming is no easy task in the harsh northern climate. In the early sixties, about a third of the workforce was still employed in the farming sector; by 1970 their share was down to about one quarter. By then Finland was an emerging industrial society with a clear majority of the workforce in services and industry.

For many years, Finland's main exports came from its vast forests in the form of raw timber, wood products, pulp and paper. Many other industrial branches, however, were also expanding, including shipbuilding, cables, technology for the paper industry, and electronics. Industrial growth was fuelled by the steady market in the neighbouring Soviet Union.

A dramatic change has been taking place since the late 1980s. The government took a deliberate decision to turn the country into a high-tech society ready for the challenges of the information age. In 1984 Finland's total research and development input was about 1 per cent of GDP, as against almost 3 per cent in the United States and Japan.

Ten years later, Finland's R&D input had already overtaken that of the US and had reached the Japanese level. In addition to an intensified focus on R&D, the programme includes a plan to connect all Finnish schools to the Internet by the year 2000.

The change is reflected in the share of Finnish exports accounted by high-tech goods. Around 5 per cent in 1988, ten years later this figure was up to 15 per cent, and high-technology thus represented the largest export segment. The value of high-tech exports first exceeded that of imports in 1995, and the gap has been widening ever since. By the end of the twentieth century, Finland was one of the most highly-developed countries of the European Union.

▶ Well over half of Finland's inhabitants, including many schoolchildren, have a mobile phone of their own.

▶ Teamwork is the order of the day at school.

Education

Finland has a system of compulsory education for all children between the ages of 7 and 17. No tuition is charged. The school system ensures virtually a 100 per cent literacy rate. Finnish is one of the easiest languages to learn to write, as there is almost complete matching between pronunciation and spelling, with one letter for one phoneme.

All children must attend comprehensive school for nine years. After that several avenues of further education are available, ranging from vocational school to upper secondary, followed by college and university. All stages of education – including university – are free of charge for students.

There are about twenty universities and colleges. Gaining admission is usually difficult. Entrance examinations are held in the summer, and the selection is normally based on a combination of performance at school and in the entrance exams. In additional to the formal school system, an extensive network of publicly and privately run institutes offer many opportunities for adult education.

High-tech industry in Finland

Finland's success in the sector of high technology did not appear all of a sudden from nowhere. The country has a long tradition of technological skills and training. Finland was one of the first countries in the world to set up a telephone service, and in the early days of broadcasting it had many radio and TV makers who competed successfully with foreign manufacturers. Some of these firms survived even after most of Europe's consumer electronics companies lost their mar-

▲ Finland has twenty universities, that of Helsinki being the biggest. The Helsinki University Library is considered to be the masterpiece of its architect Carl Ludvig Engel.

kets to Asian producers.

Another contributing factor has been the Finns' high standard of education. The school system is of generally high quality. Thus it has been relatively easy for the Finnish workforce to learn to apply new technologies, and for Finnish industry to find qualified engineers. Especially during the 1990s, the universities and industry have worked in close collaboration.

Much of the technological innovation is the result of this joint effort.

Pioneer technologies

Ships are not usually thought of as high-tech products, but that is exactly what modern ships are. Finland has very long traditions in shipbuilding. Shipbuilding began in Turku in 1737 and in Helsinki in 1865. Shipbuilding was the source of many of the technical skills and traditions which would later be used in other industrial sectors. The Finnish shipyards concentrated from an early date on special-purpose vessels, especially icebreakers. These ships required much basic research, and the shipyards developed many maritime innovations.

In 1990 the Norwegian company Kvaerner took over the leading Finnish shipbuilder, Masa-Yards Oy. Kvaerner is one of the world's largest builders of specialized ships. Many of the great cruise liners have been built in Helsinki by Kvaerner Masa-Yards. However, Kvaerner is looking for a new owner for its shipyards. The other Finnish shipyards have continued to produce special-purpose ships, such as research vessels, tankers, offshore platforms, and vessels for oil and gas production.

Finland's first major industry was based on the country's most important natural resource, forests. It was vital for the sector to be competitive with other countries producing paper and pulp. The Finns developed special expertise in wood-processing. This expertise later became a major export item. Finland is one of the world leaders in building paper machines and designing related industrial processes. Finnish forestry expertise is applied all over the world.

An early high-tech company was Vaisala Oy, set up by Professor Vilho Väisälä in 1936 to produce a meteorological radiosonde he had developed. The company is now

▶ The Gulf of Finland, the Gulf of Bothnia and the Baltic Sea freeze over for many months most winters. Winter traffic in Finnish waters – and in many other northern seas – is kept going by Finnish-made ice-breakers. The *Sampo* offers arctic cruises for tourists.

one of the world's leading manufacturers of electronic measurement systems for meteorology, environment, traffic safety and industrial research, exporting to more than 100 countries and with a worldwide network of distributors.

Nokia, a small town in southern Finland

In January 1998 Finland had 60 cellular phone connections per 100 inhabitants. It is no mere chance that the Finns have for many years now ranked either first or second in the world as users of cellular phones. The Helsinki-based company Oy Nokia Ab is the largest producer of cellular phones in the world.

The name Nokia is often taken to be Japanese. Who could imagine that one of the world's leading high-tech products should come from a small North European country? Nonetheless, Nokia is Finnish, and the name comes from that of a small town in southern Finland, where a small pulp mill was started back in 1865.

The company grew through expansions and mergers, becoming a wide-ranging industrial conglomerate producing paper and pulp, car tyres and rubber boots, cables, plastics and aluminium, consumer electronics and computers. An important acquisition was that of the radio and TV manufacturer Salora Oy, which provided the core facilities for the production of cellular phones, soon to be Nokia's prime asset.

Nokia came early to the cellular phone business. In the 1960s the company carried out studies of radio communications in its own laboratory. The world's first regular mobile telephone service was launched jointly by Telecom Finland and Nokia in Finland in 1972. In 1981 Nokia began to produce NMT system cellular phones in a factory next to the old Salora plant.

Ten years later Nokia entered the new GSM market by producing both phones and network support equipment. In the early 1990s the company took a strategic decision to concentrate on electronics and high-tech information technology products. Some of its other branches were sold off, including consumer electronics and personal computers. Today Nokia is quoted on all the major stock exchanges around the world.

The company has pioneered many new developments in the industry with products such as the Nokia 9000 Communicator, which is a combined cellular phone and

▼ Nokia's futuristic designs for third-generation mobile phone terminals.

palmtop computer with an Internet connection. Nokia and the Swedish company Ericsson have jointly developed the next generation GSM cellular phone system. Recently approved in Europe and Japan, this system looks set to emerge as the main international standard for cellular phones.

Vaisala and Nokia are just two examples of the structural changes taking place in the Finnish economy. Dozens of new high-tech ventures are born every year in the fields of information technology (both hardware and software), medical and environmental technology, industrial instrumentation, automation and system planning, as well as in biomedicine and genetic engineering. Finnish companies and research labs are also in the forefront in research on solar power cells.

Computers

For many years now, Finland has ranked first in the world in the use of computer networks and the Internet. Various explanations have been suggested, none of them conclusive. Perhaps it is easier for the taciturn Finns to communicate through a machine than by direct, face-to-face contact with unpredictable real people. This explanation seems as good as any other.

Part of the reason is that legislation on telecommunications has been liberal (by European standards). Companies, universities and individuals have been relatively free to experiment with technologies

▶ The Internet Café is a popular venue in downtown Helsinki. Customers can go websurfing for the price of a cup of coffee.

emerging from the United States. In 1987 Finland became the first European country to link up its universities to the Internet. At the same time, the general public were freely allowed to connect their computers to the telephone network to experiment with the new information technology.

Nokia was one of the first European companies to make personal computers. These won praise for their ergonomic design, especially in Europe. Thus Finland's industry acquired practical experience in computer manufacturing. Nokia later sold its computer unit to the Japanese-owned company ICL, which still makes computers in Finland. Meanwhile, Nokia continued to produce monitors for desktop PCs.

Finland has also made some contributions on the software side of information technology. Some of the basic theories and models of computer-based neural networks were written by a Finnish professor, Teuvo Kohonen. These have found numerous applications in computer technology, from industrial processes, character recognition and robotics to methods of statistical analysis. Neural network research is in fact one of the fastest-growing areas in computer science.

Kohonen's neural networks have been used to classify galaxies discovered with the Hubble space telescope, to analyse World Bank economic data on member countries, and to find new markets for future business. Self-organizing maps (SOM) help computers recognize speech and find likely candidates for bankruptcy among investors' clients. The Internet search engine WEBSOM is also based on Kohonen's self-organizing maps.

Linus Torvalds, a young computer science student at the University of Helsinki, wanted to use the Unix operating system on his own computer. As the commercial versions of the system were too expensive, however, he set out to write his own Unix-based operating system and placed it on the Internet to be used and further developed free of charge. His challenge was well received by the Net community, and the resulting worldwide operating system Linux has become a viable competitor to Windows and Unix.

The Helsinki Telephone Company (HPY) is the largest private telecommunications company in Finland. It initiated the Arena 2000 project to develop a virtual three-dimensional model of Helsinki. The actual model was designed by the Helsinki company Arcus Software Oy. Citizens can use their own computers to travel around the city and visit its sights, shops

▼ Linus Torvalds developed the Linux operating system when still a young student at the University of Helsinki; today the program is increasingly popular throughout the world.

and museums. They can enter a shop or department store and make purchases, or conduct business with government and city officials. The project is the first of its kind in the world to cover a whole city.

Several software companies have entered the international market. Data Fellows is the recipient of the prestigious European Information Technology Grand Prize and was shortlisted in *Data Communications Magazine* with only one other European producer as one of the Top 25 Hot Startups in its field. The company is one of the world's leading designers of anti-virus, encryption and security technology for computers, with distributors and customers practically everywhere that computers are used. Another Finnish company, Solid Information Technology, produces widely used cost-effective database systems.

The high number of home computers is reflected in everyday life. Finns are leaders in the use of computerized home banking services. They are also increasingly making use of computer-based information services related to education, public transport, weather

▲ A three-dimensional "Virtual Helsinki" is being set up on the Net in preparation for the year 2000, making it possible to attend "European City of Culture" events without even setting foot in the city.

and entertainment.

Several university departments offer open university network courses to the general public. In 1998 the Finns had the highest rate of Internet connections in the world (82 per 1,000 inhabitants), followed by Iceland (56), Norway (50), Sweden (40) and Denmark (28). The Finnish level is only matched locally in some high-tech areas of the United States.

Biomedicine

Biomedicine is another of Finland's high-tech industries. An international and industrial success story is Benecol, a new type of margarine developed by the Finnish food manufacturer Raisio Oy in cooperation with Finnish medical scientists. Raisio has granted licences to the process to some of the major international food industry companies.

▲ Leena Palotie, professor of molecular biology, has studied Finnish pathogens.

▼ The first transgenic calf was born at the Kuopio University experimental farm in December 1993.

Finland used to have the dubious distinction of being one of the countries with the world's highest death rates due to cardiovascular diseases. This was traced back partly to genetic factors and partly to the heavy traditional diet. Cardiovascular diseases became a priority for medical research in Finland, which gradually amassed a great deal of internationally recognized expertise. Extensive health campaigns, such as the internationally famous North Karelia Project, have reduced the incidence of cardiovascular diseases to moderate levels.

Cholesterol is necessary for health. An excessive cholesterol level in the blood, however, is one of the main risk factors for cardiovascular diseases. The Finns tend to have a significantly higher cholesterol count than people living in Southern Europe, whose diet contains less fatty foods and more fruit and vegetables.

Professor Tatu Miettinen of Helsinki University had the idea of using a harmless compound to replace some of the cholesterol in blood serum. Stanol, which is present in small quantities in all plants, turned out to be a suitable substance. Its yield, however, is small, and it is relatively expensive. Raisio Oy developed industrial methods for manufacturing stanol as a by-product of the paper and pulp industry, and used it as an ingredient in developing Benecol. Clinical tests have confirmed that stanol significantly lowers high levels of cholesterol in blood serum. Benecol has subsequently become a commercial success.

Dolly may have been the first cloned mammal, but Huomen (Morning) was the first mammal with a transplanted gene. Professor Juhani Jänne and his team from the University of Kuopio succeeded in 1993 in transferring a human gene to a calf. Huomen's milk contains a valuable protein used in medication for patients suffering from anaemia, cancer and AIDS. Several other Finnish research teams have mapped genes for a number of hereditary diseases.

Tele-communications

The Finnish telecommunications system is also exceptional by European standards. Most of Finland's local telephone operators have always been privately owned, and thus telecommunications have always been run as a mixed operation. There have been dozens of independent telephone companies in addition to the government-controlled company which used to form part of the Posts and Tele-communications Administration (PTT). Just as there was never any legislation to secure the government a monopoly in broadcasting, so there was never a government monopoly in telecommunications.

The government-controlled Telecom Finland changed its name in 1998 to Sonera. Plans have been laid to privatize the company, which for many years now has been just one of many competitors for customers in the Finnish telecom market. The company has played an important role in developing applications of modern information technologies.

The world's coldest place?

People tend to think of Finland as a very cold country. As it is, however, the Gulf Stream keeps the Scandinavian climate relatively mild. Thus, the average temperature in Finland is considerably warmer than in American and Asian regions at similar latitudes. Winters can be quite cold, but summers are mild and sunny. Nonetheless, for many years now Finland has held the world record for cold – in a laboratory.

The Low Temperature Laboratory of the Helsinki University of Technology is renowned for its work in low temperature physics. In the early 1970s, Professor Olli V. Lounasmaa and his research team were the first to confirm the occurrence of superfluidity in helium-3, as discovered by Nobel laureates David Lee, Robert Richardson and Douglas Osheroff.

The Finnish team developed new methods for observing helium-3 at temperatures just one thousandth of a degree above absolute zero. These observations have

▲ The northern elements are the focus of intense study. The Helsinki University of Technology (actually located in Espoo) has a cryogenics laboratory and Sodankylä a research centre that studies the Northern lights. The Arktikum science centre in Rovaniemi presents exhibitions on life in the polar regions. The centre also features sections for research, information and education.

helped understand some of the physical processes in the very early universe, just after the Big Bang.

The work done at the laboratory has also given rise to practical applications in brain research. Professor Riitta Hari's brain research team has developed and applied a new neuromagnetic research technique called MEG. The method allows totally noninvasive studies of the brain functions of healthy individuals while awake, providing highly accurate spatial resolution and millisecond time resolution. The results have proved extremely useful for medical purposes as well as for studies in linguistics and human perception.

In addition to the studies done

at the Low Temperature Laboratory, brain research has been carried out at the University of Helsinki's BioMag Laboratory. Dr Risto Ilmoniemi and his team have developed a method for magnetic stimulation of the brain. Professor Risto Näätänen has used the method to differentiate direct brain reactions to different sounds. The results have direct implications for our understanding of spoken language and of potential hearing defects in newborn babies. Näätänen's brain analysis system, called MMN (Mismatch Negativity), is now used by many laboratories around the world for scientific and clinical studies.

Finland in space?

To be sure, there are no Finnish astronauts; nor does Finland have a space programme of its own. However, as a member of the European Space Agency (ESA), the country is an active partner in space science projects.

Finnish instruments have gone into space on Russian, NASA and ESA flights. Thus, the Cassini-Huygens Probe, a joint ESA-NASA project to study Saturn and its moon Titan, carries a Finnish-made radar altimeter as well as instruments for pressure and plasma studies. Finnish scientists have also participated in the analysis of some NASA programmes. They carried out chemical analyses of some of the first moon rocks, and analysed the physiological tests made during the Columbia flight in spring 1998.

The Finnish media

Compared with the United States, European countries have tended towards a higher degree of government control of the media. Even Europe, however, has had a great variety of arrangements for ownership and control, ranging from full government control to an American-type decentralized media system. Finland has had perhaps the most decentralized communication system in Europe.

The Finns are exceptional media users. In most developed countries, TV viewing has increased, while reading has decreased. Not so in Finland: since the introduction of television in the 1950s, the number of newspapers, periodicals and books published has increased, and so has their readership. If the international rankings of media usage and newspaper, radio and TV ownership are combined, Finland holds second place in the world after Japan.

Contrary to most other countries, television viewing has increased very slowly in Finland since the early 1960s, and average viewing time is among the lowest in the industrial countries. The Americans watch 2.5 times as much TV as the Finns, and the British and Japanese about double the Finns' two hours a day. This despite the fact that in Finland the number of TV sets per family is among the highest in the world.

Moreover, for a European country, Finland has a large number of TV channels offering a wide variety of programmes.

The Finnish press has always been privately owned. The Finns are great newspaper readers. If we combine all the international statistics on reading – newspapers, periodicals, books and library services – the Finns are world champions. In 1996, for a total population of five million, there were 226 newspapers, 56 of them dailies. Finland had the third largest circulation of dailies in the world after Norway and Japan.

The leading communication company is Sanoma Oy, the publisher of *Helsingin Sanomat*, one of the leading newspapers in Scandinavia and, indeed, one of the world's quality papers. The same company also publish-

▼ A wide range of newspapers are published in Finnish or Swedish. During an average working week, Finnish 12-to-69-year-olds spend 8$\frac{1}{2}$ hours following the media.

es the evening paper *Ilta-Sanomat*, as well as a number of periodicals and magazines. It also owns WSOY (Finland's largest book publisher), the Channel 4 television network and Helsinki Television, which operates the country's largest cable TV system.

Magazine publishers include Yhtyneet Kuvalehdet, a large group owned by Otava Publishing Company. Among other Finnish publishing companies, Tammi now belongs to the Swedish group Bonniers. Otava and Gummerus are family-owned publishing houses. The Finns are avid readers, of books as well as of newspapers and magazines. Unlike most other countries, newspapers and magazines are generally sold by subscription.

Broadcasting operations were started in Finland by radio amateurs in the 1920s. The first radio companies were all private. In 1934 the government-controlled Finnish Broadcasting Company (Yleisradio Ab or YLE) was formed from an existing private company, and it bought up all the other private companies. The country never actually had a statutory radio or TV monopoly, although between 1933 and 1955 YLE was the only player in the broadcasting business. Since 1955 there have again been several competing broadcasting enterprises.

In 1955 students of the Helsinki University of Technology set up a private TV company called TESVISIO. A year later YLE started TV broadcasts, sharing its channel with another private company, Oy MTV Ab. In 1963 YLE bought up TESVISIO. New private TV companies have been established since 1995.

In 1998 there were two national channels operated by YLE and the private channels MTV3 (which has nothing to do with the international music channel MTV) and Channel 4, which is owned by Sanoma Oy. In addition, there was a privately operated local channel in the city of Tampere.

Cable television was introduced in Finland in the early 1970s. Most of the companies were small local cable systems. There are some more extensive systems, however, the largest being the Helsinki systems owned by Sanoma Oy.

In addition to the YLE network of radio stations, there are numerous private radio companies. Their number varies with shifting business fortunes, but is typically between 40 and 60. They are nearly all financed by advertisers; there are only a couple of small non-commercial private radio stations.

Finnish broadcasting technology has always been in the forefront of development. YLE was one of the first companies to adopt FM radio after the Second World War, and it is now actively planning to enter a new digital age in radio and TV services.

The Modern
Welfare State

Social security

The construction of Finland's present social policy began in the immediate postwar years. The key reform of this period was the Child Benefit Act of 1948, designed as an incentive for having children. By 1949 welfare expenditure had risen to an average Nordic level, accounting for 10% of GNP. The real expansion of the welfare state, however, did not come until the years of economic transition in the 1960s and '70s. Whereas in the 1940s over half of the population made a living from farming, by the 1970s their proportion was down to 18% and by the 1990s to a mere 8%. Meanwhile, the number of people working in industry and in services, especially trade and communications, increased. The futures report of the Finnish government suggests that Finland might lead the EU in the shift to the information society, acting as the Union's "information laboratory". As President Martti Ahtisaari likes to point out, the Finns are experts on social change and transition, having passed through abrupt changes in occupational structure, independence, the Second World War, the resettlement of 420,000 Karelians evacuated from territory ceded to the Soviet Union following the war, and postwar reconstruction – all in the space of one century. The Finns' best expertise, according to Ahtisaari, lies in their ability to adapt to rapid changes and in their determination to build a just society.

Economic growth and structural change took place in Finland in the 1960s at a rate unprecedented in European history. With the disintegration of the social safety net once provided by a predominantly rural society, new demands were made on social policy. Several reforms were undertaken in the 1960s. Old-age and disability pension systems were set up for the private sector in the early years of the decade. The most important reform in health care was the Sickness Insurance Act of 1964. The purpose of the Housing Production Act of 1966 was to stimulate the construction of housing with low-interest loans. These reforms illustrate the way the former concept of poor relief gave way to a system of social security managed jointly by the State and local authorities. The express aims of the new social policy were the welfare of all citizens and a more equitable distribution of the national income.

Until 1993, Finland's income policy, taxation and social security all contributed to reducing income differences. Since then, however, the trend has been reversed. Although no radical reforms have been carried out in basic social security, certain benefits have been reduced or access to them has been restricted on the grounds that public spending must be cut to fight the recession. At the same time, the production of public services has been reorganized, as local authorities increasingly complement their own services with services purchased from the private sector.

Social Security in the 1990s

Finland is not Europe's biggest spender on social services in terms of proportion to GDP, but it is among the leaders. It is a Nordic welfare state, which means that the State guarantees its citizens a certain minimum standard of living. The difference compared with social security systems in other countries is that to be eligible for social security a person does not have to have a family, be gainfully employed or possess Finnish citizenship; it is intended for all residents.

Finland's current social legislation is based on the insurance principle, covering disability due to illness or accident as well as maternity, unemployment and care of the elderly. Moreover, benefits paid include child benefits, student grants, housing allowance and child home care allowance.

The social service system includes day-care and various forms of institutional care. Individuals unable to earn a living by any other means are entitled to social assistance. In the 1990s, the volume of social expenditure attained one third of GNP.

The interesting question for both Finland and the EU as a whole is what kind of social policy model the Union will adopt in the future, and whether the social security systems of the Member States will converge as a result or whether they will retain their individual systems and forms of organization.

▶ Expectant mothers are entitled to maternity grants and young mothers to parental grants. Fathers also have the option of taking paid parental leave. Even Prime Minister Paavo Lipponen took a week's parental leave in 1998.

The family

The process of founding a family in Finland can be described as follows: a couple meets, they live together for a while, have a baby, and only then get married. This explains the statistically high percentage of unmarried couples living together, and the large number of children born out of wedlock. A typical photo in Finnish women's magazines is from the wedding of some celebrity, showing the bride and groom, and their little baby baptized at the same ceremony.

Indeed, 20% of all Finnish couples living together in 1997 were not married, when ten years earlier the figure was only 12%. The average age of marriage in 1997 was 33.3 for men and 30.7 for women, in both cases an increase of four years since the mid 1970s. The suggested causes of this development include changing moral standards and women's higher educational standard and career expectations.

Family size has also decreased over the last twenty years. In 1950 the average number of under 18-year-old children per family was 2.2; by 1997 it was down to 1.8.

60 723 children were born in Finland in 1997; 51% were boys. The overall fertility rate (i.e. the average number of children borne by one woman) was 1.8, and the average child-bearing age was 29.9. The birth rate in the 1990s differs from previous years in two respects. On the one hand, the birth rate among married and cohabiting couples is rising once more; on the other hand, the proportion of childless single women is also on the rise.

Divorces have also increased in Finland over the last twenty years. It is estimated that nearly one in four marriages end in divorce. For example, 29% of all marriages contracted in 1975 have ended in divorce. Finland heads European divorce statistics together with the Scandinavian countries and Britain. The result is an increasing number of single parents and "recycled"

▼ A family picnic in the park. The Finnish summer is relatively short, so the Finns try to make the most of every sunny day.

▲ Following graduation exercises, divine service is held in the Cathedral for the new Ph.D.'s and M.A.'s from the Helsinki University Faculty of Philosophy. Note that there are more women than men in the procession.

families, i.e. families in which one or both of the parents have children from a previous relationship.

The average family size in Finland is 2.2 persons. Farmers' families are the largest, 3.4 on average, while students (1.4) and pensioners (1.5) have the lowest average (1995 statistics). The two-provider model is typical. The Finnish family thus differs from the typical Continental family in that women have an equally strong role as providers as men. Research suggests that this is due as much to financial necessity – in particular the high cost of housing – as to women's high standard of education and career consciousness. Rents are high and one person rarely earns enough to buy an apartment or house. In the countries of Western Europe, Finland has long been second to Sweden in terms of women's participation rate in the workforce, which reached 80% just before the re-

cession. Moreover, it is significant that compared with Sweden, women's part-time work is rare in Finland. Only 15% of Finnish women work part-time, whereas the figure in other EU countries is between 30 and 40%.

Surveys also show, however, that the younger generation of women (born in the 1940s or after) do not work merely for economic reasons, but also value their own individual needs, training and career. The feminist movement has called for action to enforce equality both at work and at home, particularly citing the fact that women have

wages: the difference in men's and women's wages narrowed from 30 to 20% between 1990 and 1995.

Increasing equality has brought changes in the traditional family roles of father and mother. Here, however, there is a generation gap. Surveys show that young men participate much more frequently in household chores than their fathers did. The difference in time spent doing housework has narrowed, though it has not disappeared, over the last twenty years. According to time studies, under 35-year-old women spend some 3 $^1/_2$ hours a day and men 2 hours a day on domestic chores.

The term "new fatherhood" has been coined to describe the change in men's role. This primarily means a new relationship to children. Fathers of the younger generation spend a good deal more time with their children than the older generation did. The father is present at 70% of all childbirths, and accompanies the mother to prenatal and child welfare clinics more frequently than before.

▲ Sirkka Hämäläinen has made an impressive career in the predominantly male banking world: formerly Governor of the Bank of Finland, she is now a member of the Executive Board of the European Central Bank.

an equally high standard of education as men – indeed, in some fields, higher – and participate equally in working life. Statistics indicate that women have in fact already narrowed the gap at work. Nonetheless, among the leading figures in the business world and politics, only two to three per cent are women. Women are better represented, though nowhere near equally, among the scientific and cultural elite. A woman's career tends to stop at the lower or middle echelons of the hierarchy. A slight advance has been recorded recently in

Support for families with children

Mothers and families with children are supported in many ways with public funds and services. A comparison made of family support in the countries of Western Europe shows that Finland and Norway offer the widest range of benefits for families.

In Finland pregnant women

are entitled to maternity allowance for 105 working days, 30-50 days before and the rest after childbirth. The maternity allowance is followed by parental allowance, payable for a period of 158 days to either the mother or the father. The idea is to promote equality and to permit the mother to work at least part-time while the father looks after the baby. Few fathers have availed themselves of this opportunity, however. Fewer than half of all fathers opted for any parental allowance at all in 1996, and even those who did only took 14 days of parental leave on average.

The most important form of family support is every child's right to day-care, for this is what makes it possible for young mothers to work. Local authorities are required by law to offer each child a place in either a day-care centre or with a family day-care provider. The latter are on the local authority's payroll. In 1996, day-care centres in Finland looked after 140 629 children, and a further 76 841 were in family day-care; local authorities thus provided day-care services for a total of over 200 000 children. Most Finns, regardless of social status or income, consider either form of day-care to be acceptable for their children. Fees vary, depending on the family's income and number of children.

Municipal day-care is not, however, the only child care service available. Efforts have been made during the last ten years to provide more choice for parents. Home care support is paid for child care given at home or in a private day-care centre. Families receive this benefit until the child reaches the age of three. The size of the benefit varies from one municipality to the next, ranging from FIM 2 000 to 3 000 a month for a family with two children. This corresponds to about one third of

▶ Finnish men do their fair share of housework these days. Young fathers also spend a great deal of time with their children.

▲ The day-care centre provides children with social skills and their first friends. Statutory free meals for children are a feature unique to Finnish day-care centres and schools.

women's average earnings.

Home care support and parental allowance are both treated as taxable income. The child benefit, however, is exempt from tax. It is paid for each under 17-year-old, staggered according to the number of children in the family. Thus, the allowance for the first child in 1997 was FIM 535 and the maximum allowance, payable for the fifth child, was FIM 1023.

According to a study done by the research services of the European Commission, Finland's excellent basic benefits, payable in a variety of forms, give Finnish families with children substantial purchasing power compared with families in similar circumstances in other countries of the European Union.

Aging and social security

Finnish women had a life expectancy of 80.5 years and men of 73.4 years in 1997. Owing to increasing life expectancy and a decreasing number of children, the centre of the age pyramid is expanding.

Among Finland's 5.1 million inhabitants in 1997, the largest age group consisted of 45–49-year-old "baby boomers" and the smallest of 20–24-year-olds. Finland is "greying", a common trend throughout Europe. In 1998 the proportion of over 65s was 14%; it is expected that by 2030 almost one Finn in four will be over 65. According to projections, the population will reach 5.3 million in 2020, after which it will begin to dwindle. This change will require increased public spending on the elderly, leading to a growing burden for the younger generations having to provide for them. The traditional class conflict is in fact being replaced by a generation conflict, as illustrated by the current debate on the way Finland's public debt, although not among the highest even in Europe, is being saddled on younger generations. On the other hand, the older generations defend their pension benefits, which for some are quite high, against the criticism of the young with the argument that they financed their own pensions by paying high contributions.

The pensionable age in Finland is between 60 and 65. What with early and individual retirement schemes, disability pensions and unemployment pensions, however, the average age of retirement is actually 59, unusually low by European standards. Suggested reasons include attitudes at workplaces, strenuous duties and attractive benefits. Significantly, both basic and earnings-related pension benefits are among the best in the OECD. Fully vested pension rights amounting to 60% of earnings can be attained with a 40-year career. Owing to the generous public pension system, private schemes – which are common

elsewhere in Europe – have been relatively insignificant until quite recently. The recession of the 1990s, however, boosted their popularity.

The broad scope of the welfare state is also reflected in legal provisions on the obligations of the authorities and the family regarding old people. The law in the Nordic countries does not recognize any other family obligations than those of parents towards their children. The legal obligation to look after one's parents was repealed in 1970. To this extent, Finland and the other Nordic countries differ from the rest of Europe. The primary responsibility of the State does not, however, mean that people neglect their parents. Studies have shown that parents in need of assistance receive 70% of the help they need from their offspring if they live in the same area.

It is unusual, however, for aging mothers or fathers to move in with their children. Old-age homes are available for elderly people unable to look after themselves. In 1997, 11% of the over-75 population lived in such homes. In recent years, municipal and private service flats have been set up in many places, and in 1997 some 6% of the over-75s

▶ Every effort is made to enable aging people to live at home for as long as possible. The local authorities provide nursing, home care and catering services, charged in proportion to the recipient's income. Some also provide a taxi service for disabled senior citizens.

lived in such flats. Moreover, local authorities arrange domestic help for aging people. In 1997 an average 20% of over-75s received such help every week. The general policy aim is for everyone to live at home as long as she or he is capable of doing so, and to guarantee all those who must be moved to an old people's a home a room of their own and individualized care.

Health care and sickness insurance

The emphasis in Finnish health policy is on the availability and equitable allocation and use of services. The goal is to make public health services equally available to all, regardless of social status, income or place of residence.

Primary responsibility for providing health services rests with the local authorities. Most municipalities have at least a health centre to provide basic services. The country is divided into 21 hospital districts which provide specialized services and operate hospitals. Moreover, the universities run central hospitals which provide medical care and train physicians. Finland's health spending is average by OECD standards: in 1997 overall expenditure on health services was about 7% of GDP and 16% of all social expenditure. The only fee charged by health centres is an annual enrolment fee of FIM 100. Moreover, public sickness insurance covers part of any other medical costs. Hospitals charge patients FIM 125 per night and FIM 100 per outpatient visit. The average replacement ratio provided by sickness and accident insurance (allowance per gross earnings) is just under 70% of annual income.

In terms of health indicators, Finland is one of the leading European countries. Infant mortality (i.e. deaths of under 1-year-olds) was 0.39% in 1996, lowest in the world.

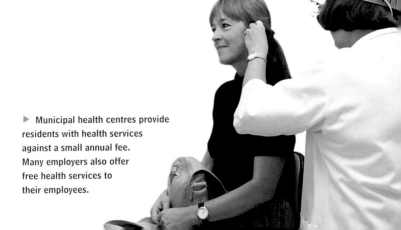

▶ Municipal health centres provide residents with health services against a small annual fee. Many employers also offer free health services to their employees.

▶ Child health centres monitor the health and development of children closely.

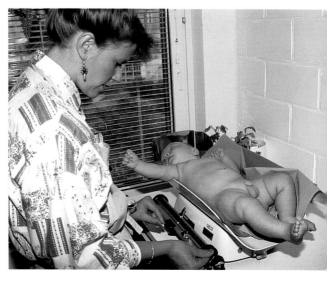

Prenatal care and child welfare clinics have a long history in Finland. The Mannerheim League for Child Welfare was founded back in 1920 to promote the safety of children, young people and families. Although at the time the public welfare system did not extend to child health care and protection, the League promptly set up a nationwide network of clinics providing advice and aid to expectant mothers and families with children. These clinics are now run by the local authorities.

Various forms of preventive and rehabilitative action are also available. One of the keystones of preventive health policy is cancer screening aimed at detecting the disease at an early stage. Mortality from cancer is low compared with most other countries. The results have been so encouraging that in the 1990s health policy has focused increasingly on prevention and rehabilitation.

Joblessness and unemployment benefits

The recession caught Finland, like many other European countries, unprepared. Although the public debt is still growing, however, the fact that for several years GDP growth has been between 3 and 5.7 per cent is a sign that the worst is over. Unemployment in Finland, however, still remains second highest in the EU after Spain. The jobless rate, which hit an all-time high of 18% in the early years of the recession, has come down to 10.9% according to the 1999 labour force survey, and according to some forecasts it should decrease further to 8% by about 2005. By the 2010s Finland is expected to be suffering from a labour shortage.

According to Statistics Finland's consumer survey, consumer confidence in the economy has strengthened recently. Over half of the population ex-

▲ The unemployment rate in 1999 was around 11%. The employment offices help job-seekers find work and, if appropriate, place them in training. Self-help is still the best way to find a job, however.

pect both the economy and the unemployment situation to improve.

Even in the peak years of unemployment, there was never the kind of unrest among the unemployed as there was in France, for example. Basic unemployment benefits and the housing allowance provide a sufficient standard of living, while earnings-related benefits are relatively generous (between 60% and 66% of working income). The government has made efforts to upgrade the skills of the unemployed with adult education and other training. Under-25s must take part in some form of training in order to qualify for benefits.

Those who do not qualify for unemployment allowance receive social assistance providing basic subsistence. Combined with the housing allowance, this benefit amounted to approximately one third of the average Finnish wage in 1997. Although this is quite high, beneficiaries' income is just under half of the median income, which is comparable to other European countries.

Income and taxation

The principal source of income is wage work for 49% of all Finnish households; agricultural or business income for 10%, pensions for 28%, unemployment benefits for 9% and other forms of income (including study grants, child home care allowance, etc.) 5%.

Compared with the United

States and most West European countries, Finland has a very even income distribution. The average monthly wage for men is FIM 12,358 and for women FIM 10,201. The difference is at least partly due to the fact that women and men tend to work in different fields; according to Statistics Finland's data, the status of an occupation and its wage level do not always match.

Taxes accounted for 47.3% of Finland's GNP in 1997, which was not significantly higher than in other European countries. Among West European countries, the gross tax rate was higher in Denmark and Sweden. The average income tax rate in Finland in 1997 was 35.8%. A family of four with two providers paid 38% tax on average in 1997. Surveys indicate that some 80% of the population consider the current tax rate excessive. As in other EU countries, there has been strong pressure for reducing taxation in recent years.

Disposable family income is reduced by progressive taxation as well as by income transfers dictated by social policy considerations. It is worth noting that university graduates have higher earnings in proportion to the rest of the population in Finland than in most other industrialized countries. Nonetheless, Finland has the world's most even income distribution according to an OECD study from 1995. The apparent paradox is explained by the fact that progressive taxation and income transfers have a stronger equalizing effect on earnings than in most other countries. Differences in net earnings, calculated using the Gini coefficient, are smaller than in France, the United States, Germany and even Sweden.

INCOME AND STATUS OF CERTAIN OCCUPATIONS IN FINLAND

High status High income	Annual income	Low status High income
managing director	FIM 350 000	lawyer, doctor
insurance inspector	FIM 300 000	bank manager
engineer, general manager	FIM 250 000	real estate agent
reporter, computer programmer	FIM 200 000	fur farmer
class teacher, actor	FIM 150 000	plumber, carpenter
nurse	FIM 100 000	shopkeeper
kleaner, messanger	FIM 80 000	farmer, joiner
High status Low income		Low status Low income

Source: Statistics Finland. *Suomen Kuvalehti* 8.11.1996.

The Finnish way of life and cultural features

The Finnish way of life, as expressed by standard of living, leisure habits, friendships, customs and events, has both general European aspects and distinctively Finnish features. Differences between social classes are much smaller than in, say, France or Britain. There are no salient differences in the clothes people wear; nor do their leisure occupations differ sharply. Housing space, however, is clearly a function of income, and differentiates the Finns more than any other lifestyle indicator.

According to 1996 statistics, 61.3% of all dwellings are owner-occupied. The top income bracket live in spacious row houses or single-family houses with 4 to 5 rooms on average. The average living space per person is 33.4 square metres (1996). Thus, although Finland places near the top in Europe with respect to other indicators of prosperity, the Finns' homes are small by West European standards. One of the explanations proffered for this lack of space is that the severe climate makes construction expensive. The government supports housing construction by granting interest subsidies for housing loans. Moreover, 185,000 households received housing support and 989,000 citizens received tax deductions for mortgage interest payments in 1997.

According to statistics provided by the 1996 standard-of-living survey, households spent 27.9% of their income on housing, 17% on food, restaurant meals and beverages, 20% on transport, telecommunications and travel, and 8.3% on recreation and leisure. Compared with similar statistics from the 1970s, housing expenses had increased and those

▼ Houses in the country tend to have more living space than the often rather cramped flats in urban apartment blocks. According to an old saw, "Finns want to live in a house of their own, by a lakeside in the centre of town".

on food and beverages had decreased.

Differences of lifestyle in Finland in fact have more to do with the generation gap than with class divisions or income groups. As a result of the rapid postwar industrialization process, different generations have had entirely different experiences. J.P. Roos has studied the Finnish generations of the twentieth century. First came the war generation, who were born at the turn of the century. The hardships and shortages they experienced explain their ascetic, thrifty way of life. The second, the generation of postwar reconstruction and economic growth, was born in the 1920s and '30s and witnessed Finland's rapid industrialization. This generation was characterized by entrepreneurship and a pioneer spirit. The third generation was born during the war or just after it in the 1940s. This transitional generation ex-

The fells of Lapland are among the Finns' favourite holiday destinations. Many also regularly go cross-country skiing near their home.

perienced the rapid improvement in Finland's living standards and saw the meteoric rise of technology. This generation is still known as the baby boomers or the Bulge, as owing to the high postwar birth rate it is much larger than other age groups. According to Antti Karisto, this generation was marked by social betterment and expansion of the education system, and formed the economic and political elite. It also differed from the previous generation in that it saw Finland's transformation from a predominantly rural culture to an urban one. Its members, who recently turned fifty or are about to do so, see themselves as the vanguard of modern society.

The next generation, born in the '50s, is perhaps no longer united by a common background to such a degree. This is the suburban generation of individualistic young adults, highly educated, fashion-conscious, consumerist, well versed in the new technologies, at home in a world of mobile phones and the Internet. According to a gallup poll, under 35-year-old Finns tend to place a greater emphasis on social ethics than their seniors: they think people should do their work properly and expect honesty from politicians. The younger generation is clearly also more critical about society, while materialism is on the wane.

The standard-of-living survey carried out once every ten years provides interesting data on the hobbies and interests of the Finns. Here are a few examples from the most recent survey (1991):

The Finns spend an average $2^{1}/_{2}$ hours a day watching television. TV series and entertainment programmes have the highest viewer ratings, followed by newscasts and sports events. Sports are a crucial ingredient of Finnish culture.

What do the Finns eat?

Through Swedish and Russian influence Finnish cuisine has always been international, mainly European. Domestic ingredients are often applied to new recipes. A touch of the West, another of the East, mixed with the traditions from Lapland; this is the blend that makes up the Finnish cusine.

The Finnish culinary year

In *January* the Finns warm up with soup, roasts and casseroles. The seasonal fish is burbot, which is generally served in soup, but can also be stewed or fried. Its roe is among the most highly appreciated. Salt cured roe is served with sour cream or whipped cream, chopped onions and boiled liver, and black pepper or allspice.

On *February* 5, the anniversary of national poet Johan Ludvig Runeberg, the flags come out and everyone eats Runeberg tartlets. Shrovetide fare is also seasonal: pea soup, *blini* and special Shrovetide buns.

	Women, %	Men, %
watch TV every day	69	75
take exercise at least once a week	84	80
have read at least one book during the last month	80	70
during the last months, have been to:		
– a concert	39	27
– the theatre	46	28
– an art exhibition	50	38

Children faithfully watch their own TV programmes and videos. Many parents also read aloud to their children.

▲ A medley of fish roe with sour cream and minced onions tastes delicious on *blini* or toast.

Easter comes in *March* or *April*. Desserts have pride of place on the table: *mämmi*, a special Finnish delicacy consecrated by the European Union, eggs filled with mouthwatering mignon chocolate, the traditional Orthodox red eggs, *pasha*, *kulitsa* and *baba* cake steeped in rum.

May is the spawning season of perch, pike, bream and Baltic herring, all of which are widely available. Herring is *de rigueur* for May Day, as are *tippaleipä* fritters and mead.

The summer holidays begin in *June*, when many Finns set out for the country. The new, tender shoots of rhubarb are brought in from the garden, and the first new potatoes and garden strawberries appear in shops. The whole country celebrates Midsummer with a bonfire and a sauna bath. Bologna rings and home-brewed ale or beer are on the menu. The men bring out their outdoor grills and smoke ovens for the summer.

They say the whole country

shuts down in *July,* when the holiday season really gets under way. The wild strawberries, blueberries, Arctic brambles and cloudberries ripen. The "big" question of the day is whether the blueberry pie should have a shortbread crust or a leavened one. The mushroom-crazy nation picks its first ceps and chanterelles. The crayfish season begins July 21 at noon. That very night, gourmets pay a fortune for the precious crustaceans, downed to the accompaniment of vodka and drinking songs borrowed from the Swedes.

August is raspberry and currant time. The shooting season begins with pigeon, followed by duck. This is also the season for grilled lamprey, and friends compare notes at fishmongers' and market booths. Domestic pastrycooks delight the family with apple pie.

In *September,* hunters take aim at hare and, a little later, at elk and deer. The last berries of the forest ripen: lingonberry, cranberry and, in Lapland, black crowberry. The summer homes are locked up, and the pickling season ends.

All along the west and south coast, *October* is the time of the Baltic herring market, with many festive sideshows. The islanders and fishermen bring in their autumn produce: Baltic herring prepared in every possible way, juices, breads and specialty fare. This is a harvest celebration, rather like a muted carnival, as is the reindeer round-up in Lapland, when some of the herd is picked out for slaughter.

The hunting season ends in *November;* St. Martin's goose and "Little Christmas" parties with *glögg* (mulled wine) are the order of the day.

The big decision in *December* is whether to serve ham or turkey for the Christmas Eve dinner. The traditional accompaniments include boiled peas and prunes and casseroles made with swede, carrot or sweetened potato. These are usually preceded by a fish entrée, such as Baltic herring with various kinds of sauce, pickled herring, *gravlax* and the traditional herring salad. Prunes are served in various forms, including blancmange and prune-filled Christmas tarts.

What is the symbol of Finnish cuisine?

Rye bread, butter, milk and buttermilk? Potatoes? *Kalakukko* and *mämmi*? Or a certain sausage ring that the TV

▼ Fresh-piched blueberries and milk are a special summer treat.

commercials say make the Finns happy?

In recent years, what with the flood of information, marketing, tourism and new ideas about healthy nutrition, the culinary symbols of Finland have changed. The Finns favour a light, healthy diet; they are careful about what they put in their mouths. Their motto is "eat well, feel good." In addition to their own traditional dishes, they eat "world food." Consumers are "omnivorous": they like to prepare everything from scratch, but will also settle for convenience foods on occasion. Lightness, low sodium content and low fat content are more important qualities to many than flavour. The demand for organically grown Finnish raw materials is on the rise.

The Finns appreciate fine cuisine, but consume it in moderation. Gastronomic delights and healthy habits go hand in hand. The next millennium is expected to bring a renewed acceptance of epicureanism, a quest for gourmet experiences.

Along with the new thinking, traditional foods such as sausage are still popular. But the sausage has changed: it is meatier and tastier than ever. The animal fat in sausage is replaced nowadays with healthier vegetable fats, and enriched with ingredients that have beneficial health effects. One such additive is pine bark flour, produced in the context of a project supported by the EU.

The triumph of functional, healthful ingredients continues. The most Finnish among these is rye, which has been scientifically demonstrated to improve well-being and reduce cholesterol and the risk of coronary disease. It turns out that the Finns have in fact always had a healthy diet, thanks in part to wholemeal products (rye, barley, oats).

The researchers' list of functional products is still growing. The best-known Finnish innovation in this category has a worldwide reputation: Benecol is a cholesterol-reducing vegetable fat reputed as a remedy for all ills.

▲ ▲ *Schnapps* and cheerful drinking songs are essential elements of the crayfish ritual.

▲ Salmon cooked over an open fire.

A carefully chosen, light diet

Mealtimes have changed with the times. Finnish families have many other interests besides TV. Since the hobbies of family members reduce their time together in the afternoons and evenings, the main family meal is now breakfast. It's a full meal for the Finns. Porridges are in high regard, and many families also go for muesli, bran, cereals, yoghurt and milk. Bread is a must, and the toast is increasingly of the wholemeal variety. Light margarine is a serious alternative to butter. Many households have exchanged the lightly roasted Finnish coffee for darker roasts, imbibed in Continental style from a glass, often as *café au lait*. Finland is a world leader in coffee consumption statistics, but tea is also gaining ground. And naturally the daily dose of vitamin C is provided in the form of juice, fruit, vegetables or berries.

Canteen meals in educational institutions and offices contain an increasing proportion of vegetables. Both schools and homes do their best to follow the recommendations of health experts, giving pride of place to grain products, potatoes and vegetables.

Most of those who pack their own lunch or buy a quick snack will supplement their lunch with salads, vegetables and fruit.

Apart from water, many still drink milk, buttermilk or beer with their meals, while the small but growing group of winelovers have discovered to their relief that a glass or two of red wine with lunch is no longer frowned upon, even on a daily basis.

Dinner time will depend on the family members' working hours and hobbies, but the weekend is the time when most families gather around the same table. They prepare this meal together, for in many families everyone takes an interest in cooking, and baking is "in".

The cup that cheers

"It's time for a cup of coffee" is a remark you hear often in Finland. Cafés can be found in libraries, theatres, even in hairdresser's shops. Afternoon coffee is often accompanied by *pulla* buns, Danish pastries or cake. The "coffee party" is still part of most Finns' lives, but the "seven sweets" served with coffee at major anniversaries have given way to a mix between a smorgasbord and dessert buffet. Savoury tidbits, salads sandwiches, "sandwich cake" and pasties are served along with the obligatory sweet cake or tart.

Big family celebrations are increasingly entrusted to caterers. The presentation varies from region to region, but local specialties are always prominently featured. The *karjalanpiirakka* (thin rye pasty with potato or rice filling) has been adopted over the years by the whole nation. Large quantities of this delicacy are produced industrially, but these do not hold a candle to the homemade real thing. The best *piirakka* are still fashioned by hand by Karelian matrons, baked in a traditional bread ovens and served with *munavoi*, a delicious mixture of hardboiled egg mashed with butter.

▶ Coffee time.

The modern Finnish pub

The new age has brought rural sales outlets to many localities (generally along main roads). They offer farm-baked bread and sausage, grain products, cold meats, honey, and eggs laid by free-range hens. This is part of a new phenomenon known as culinary tourism. The old village bars have virtually disappeared, and the business of feeding travellers has been taken over by service station restaurants.

While fast food chains are spreading throughout the country, the fine restaurants keep abreast with the times. The leading chefs are well-versed in the uses of raw ingredients available in their own region, and are adept at adjusting them to Finnish tastes.

A good indicator of how well Finland is keeping up is the success of Finnish chefs in international gastronomy competitions. Fifth place in the Bocuse d'Or in Lyon is one of their more notable recent achievements. Although they may look abroad for inspiration, the self-confidence and patriotism of Finnish chefs are on the rise. They are striving to make the most of homegrown ingredients.

A chef preparing a representative Finnish buffet might select the following delicacies: fish roe with accompaniments, *gravlax* or smoked fish, smoked ham or lamb, soft white cheese, beetroot-carrot-herring salad and Finnish vegetables, and dark rye bread. The main course might be fish from one of the thousands of lakes or prime beef or game, served with wild mushrooms, potatoes and organically grown vegetables. All this is followed up with a selection of Finnish cheese and, for dessert, fresh berries from the forest or garden, topped with a dollop of ice cream.

The final touch is provided by coffee and a glass of one of Finland's exquisite berry liqueurs.

Sports

Finland's countryside is unspoilt, an irresistible invitation to get up and go. Running, skiing, swimming, rowing, orienteering and cycling are popular sports, combining the joy of physical exertion with the great outdoors. There are also numerous indoor sports complexes to choose from.

The most popular forms of outdoor recreation include walking, cycling, cross-country skiing and swimming. Among team sports, floorball has won a large following over the last ten years or so. The classic team sports are (European) football in summer and ice hockey in winter. Finland's national sport *pesäpallo* is a variety of American baseball, a favourite summer sport especially in rural areas and in the smaller towns. Recent additions to the repertoire include snowboarding in winter, rollerblade, rollerboard and 'Nordic walking' (supported by poles) in the summer.

Many mass events are held in Finland. A traditional one is the *Jukolan viesti*, an all-night orienteering relay, accompanied by the *Venlojen viesti,* a similar event for women's teams. For two days, thousands of contestants camp out near the starting area, where things sometimes get as crowded as at a rock festival. A rather different event is the Helsinki Cup, a soccer jamboree for young players that attracts over 800 teams from around the world. Thousands of Finns take part in the biggest cross-country skiing event, the 75-kilometre Finlandia race. Most of the competitors are there just to enjoy the exercise and companionship, but it's serious business for the top contenders.

▼ The Sulkava rowing regatta attracts almost 10 000 participants every July.

The crucial moment in the history of Finnish competitive sports came during the 1912 Olympic Games in Stockholm. Nationalist feeling ran high at the time, and the movement for independence from Russia was gaining momentum. An inkling of things to come was provided by the opening ceremony, where the Finnish team marched behind its own name-board, separate from the Russian team. The games themselves were a huge success for Finland, which won nine gold medals. Hannes Kolehmainen, the first "Flying Finn", became the national hero by winning the 5000 and 10 000 metres and the cross-country race. Kolehmainen was succeeded in this role by Paavo Nurmi, the all-time champion of long-distance running. Nurmi won nine gold and three silver medals during his career, one of the greatest achievements in Olympic history.

The most successful athletics events for Finland have been long-distance running and javelin throwing. The javelin, in particular, has been dominated by Finns, who have won nine Olympic gold medals and numerous world championships and European championships in the event. The first major success came in 1912 in Stockholm, where the Finnish javelin team led by Julius Saaristo took all three medals. The most recent major gold medal in the event went to Heli Rantanen, who won the women's javelin in the 1996 Olympic Games in Atlanta. The Finns have been less successful in running in recent years. The last "Flying Finn" was Lasse Virén, who won both the 5000 and the 10 000 metres in the 1972 and 1976 Olympic Games. No other runner has ever taken the long-distance "double" in two consecutive Olympics.

Finns have also had a great deal of success in many contests of strength. They dominated the international wrestling scene in the early 20th century, having easily the best team in 1912 and at all the Olympics in the 1920s. Such feats are no longer possible, but the Finnish Greco-Roman wrestlers are still among the international elite. The great Finnish name in weightlifting was Kaarlo Kangasniemi, who won gold in the world championships, European championships and Olympics in the late 1960s and early '70s.

The Finns have never done so well in summer team events. They have, however, taken great strides in the "royal game", football, over the last ten years or so. Many Finnish players have been recruited by European professional teams, and have had no small success. For some years now, the brightest Finnish star in the sport has been Jari Litmanen.

The first Finnish world championship golds in swimming went to Antti Kasvio in the 200 metres freestyle and to Jani Sievinen in the 200 metres medley in 1994. Sievinen also won Olympic silver in the same event in 1996, and has set a dozen world records over the years.

The Finns have done well in many winter sports. One of the early heroes was the speed skater Clas Thunberg, also

known as "the Nurmi of the ice rink." He won a total of five golds, one silver and one bronze in Olympics, and was crowned champion of the world and of Europe many times over. Petri Kokko and Susanna Rahkamo won gold in the European championships and silver in the world championships in ice dancing in 1995.

Finland has had many heroes in Nordic skiing. The first Olympic winner was Veli Saarinen, who took gold in the men's 50 kilometres in 1932. Veikko Hakulinen was the big star in the 1950s. Eero Mäntyranta succeeded him in the '60s, winning the relay gold in the 1960 Olympics and two golds and a silver in 1964. The best athlete overall at the 1984 Winter Olympics in Sarajevo was Marja-Liisa Kirvesniemi, who won three gold medals – all the women's individual events. The Finnish Olympic winner in 1988 was Marjo Matikainen, today known as a member of the European Parliament,

▲ Finland's best footballer Jari Litmanen, here in the blue-and-white colours of the national team.

▶ Mika Myllylä made cross-country skiing history in the 1999 World Championships in Ramsau, winning three gold medals and one silver.

and in 1992 it was Marjut Lukkarinen's turn to win. Among the men, the most successful skiers today are Harri Kirvesniemi and Mika Myllylä, who won gold in the 50 kilometres in Nagano.

The Finns have been equally successful, if not more so, in ski jumping. The first Finnish Olympic champion in this discipline was Antti Hyvärinen in 1956, and since him Finns have frequently topped major events. The greatest ski jumper of all time was Matti Nykänen, who won four Olympic golds and five world championships in the 1980s. After Nykänen, the biggest names have been Toni Nieminen, who took two golds and one bronze in the 1992

▲ Mika Häkkinen, 1998 world champion in Formula One racing, and Tommi Mäkinen, world champion rally driver from 1996 to 1998.

Olympics; Ari-Pekka Nikkola, on the podium time and again in the team event; Jani Soininen, who won gold and silver in Nagano in 1998, and Janne Ahonen, world champion in 1997.

The first Finnish world championship in Alpine skiing went to Kalle Palander in the slalom event in 1999. A number of Finns are leading contenders in one of the most popular new winter events, snowboarding.

The most popular winter event of all in Finland, however, is ice hockey. The Finnish team had fairly mediocre results until 1988, when Finland took the silver medal in Calgary. The next major success came in 1992, when Finland played in the World Championship finals, though it lost to Sweden. At last in 1995, the roles were reversed. The best-known Finnish hockey players are Jari Kurri and Teemu Selänne. Kurri is in fact the most successful European player of all time in the National Hockey League, while Selänne, also known as "The Finnish Flash", has been the NHL's highest-scoring player three times.

Today's biggest Finnish stars, however, are racing drivers. Two Finns have won the most prestigious racing series of all, Formula One: Keijo ("Keke") Rosberg, crowned world champion in 1982, and Mika Häkkinen, who took the crown in 1998.

There have been many champion rally drivers from Finland. The first to become world champion was Ari Vatanen in 1981. Juha Kankkunen won the world championship no less than four times in the 1980s and '90s. This feat is about to be challenged by Tommi Mäkinen, who won the championship three times running from 1996 to 1998.

Culture

The Finns have a special respect for culture. J.V. Snellman, a 19th century statesman and the leading Finnish philosopher, wrote that a small nation's power was in its culture; it was the only means to advancement. Though a Swedish-speaker himself, Snellman was an enthusiastic propagator of the Finnish language and literature. His grand idea was the making of a unified Finnish nation; and made it was. The idea of national education spread across the social spectrum, down to the lowliest peasant. Even today, culture enjoys significant government support, the most striking results being seen in the field of music.

Architecture

Finland is a country of modern architecture. In the old days, most buildings were made of wood, and the few old houses that never burned down eventually rotted away. What is more, for centuries Finland served as a battleground, and some wars laid waste to virtually the whole country. Thus no less than 90% of all buildings date from the period of independence, i.e. from after 1917. And the homes of one third of all Finns were built less than twenty years ago.

All the same, a number of precious historical monuments have survived. There are over seventy small but well-proportioned mediaeval greystone churches, the oldest of them in Åland, near Turku and along the south coast. True, there has been some controversy of late about the age of these buildings, and it now seems as if several churches previously thought to date from the 13th century were actually built a hundred years later or so.

A few wooden churches from the 17th century have been preserved, notably at Petäjävesi, Palta-

◀ The mighty walls of Olavinlinna Castle provide a magnificent setting for the summer opera festival in Savonlinna.

▲ Senate Square, designed by Carl Ludvig Engel in the early 20th century, still serves its original purpose perfectly today. Left to right, the University, the University Library, the Cathedral and, in the foreground, the Palace of the Council of State.

mo and Keuruu. An unusual sight is Kerimäki Church, one of the world's largest wooden structures, big enough to seat a congregation of 4,000. Built in 1849, this shrine also hosts many well-attended concerts in summer.

Another interesting chapter in Finnish history is recalled by a handful of mediaeval stone castles. No trumpets of war sound from their walls today; instead, the beautifully restored castles of Turku, Häme and Olavinlinna (the home of the annual Savonlinna Opera Festival), are now dedicated to cultural pursuits.

The splendidly romantic island fortress of Suomenlinna (or Viapori) lies off the coast of Helsinki, just a short boat trip away. The "Gibraltar of the North", built by Augustin Ehrensvärd between 1710 and 1712, this was the largest construction project of its time in Scandinavia; today it is a historic site renowned throughout Europe.

Only a small number of historic homes have been preserved, although several small towns still have whole districts of wooden houses, an unusual sight in Europe. Also worth seeing are the industrial estates of the seventeenth century, the major tourist draws being Fiskars, Mustio and Ruotsinpyhtää on the south coast.

The rural Empire style of the early nineteenth century is represented notably by churches, parsonages and wooden manor houses, many of them designed by the German-born architect Carl Ludvig Engel (1776-1840). Helsinki owes a particular debt of gratitude to Engel for the fine Empire buildings fringing Senate Square: the cathedral, university, Council of State and many smaller buildings form one of Europe's most unified Neoclassical architectural settings. On the other hand, Engel can be grateful to Helsinki, for few architects in the world ever had the chance to design a whole new capital city. This, however, is exactly what Engel was ordered to do in the early 1800s by decree of the Russian Tsar.

Finland's fame as a forerunner in modern architecture dates from the rise of the Art Nouveau movement (called National Romanticism or Jugend in Finland) around 1900. The forward-looking nation, defying Russian efforts at assimi-

lation, was a hotbed for new ideas. Finns deliberately strove to establish a distinctive national culture, collecting funds for many new public buildings in a show of independence. The Finnish pavilion at the World Fair in Paris in 1900, designed by the trio Armas Lindgren (1874–1929), Herman Gesellius (1874–1916) and Eliel Saarinen (1873–1950), triggered a downright furore for Finland in Europe at the turn of the century. The Villa Hvitträsk, built by the three architects near Helsinki, was the supreme achievement of the Jugend movement, embodying its ideals of comfort, freedom and affinity with nature.

Hardly any other city in the world has preserved its Art Nou-

◀ The dining room is one of the most charming interiors in the Villa Hvitträsk. The sofa in the window niche is covered by a richly decorated weave designed by Eliel Saarinen. A lovely view of the shimmering lake below opens up from the window.

◀ Architects Raili and Reima Pietilä provided an object lesson on the potential of concrete for creating free forms in Dipoli, the Helsinki University of Technology student union building. The irregularly shaped segments of the building rise straight out of the rock.

veau quarters as intact as the Katajanokka district, the stronghold of National Romanticism in Helsinki. Another prime example of the style is Tampere Cathedral, designed by Lars Sonck (1870–1956).

The Functionalist movement was also taken very seriously by the Finns in the 1920s and '30s. Alvar Aalto (1898–1976) and Erik Bryggman (1891–1955) strove for a natural lifestyle based on the three cornerstones of reason, light and healthfulness. Bryggman's Chapel of the Resurrection in Turku is drawn with a delicate touch and makes sophisticated use of natural light; together with the Åbo Academy library, it represents Finnish Functionalist architecture at its finest.

The third golden age of Finnish architecture came in the 1950s, with Aulis Blomstedt (1906–1979) and Viljo Revell (1910–1964) among the pioneers of the new idiom. Rising from the shadows of war, Finland went through a period of reconstruction, industrialization and urbanization. New churches, schools, libraries, town halls and apartment blocks sprang up everywhere. Green suburbs were built, the "garden town" of Tapiola in Espoo showing the way. Unfortunately, the Modernist fever led to the needless destruction of much that was old and valuable.

Luminosity and light forms are still the key to Finnish architecture today, characterizing the works of architects such as Kristian Gullichsen (b. 1932) and Juha Leiviskä (b. 1936). In the buildings

ALVAR AALTO

■ The surprise winner of an architectural competition held for the Viipuri Library in the mid 1920s was a young, little-known architect by the name of Alvar Aalto. His winning design, a bold, airy combination of wood, concrete, glass and brick, was something completely new; perhaps even more surprisingly, it was carried out virtually unmodified. After the city of Viipuri was taken over by the Soviet Union following the Second World War, the library was abandoned for many years and suffered serious damage.

Aalto's next competition victory, the Paimio Sanatorium, was built between 1929 and 1933, and is another landmark in the history of modern architecture. With his architect wife Aino, Aalto worked out every detail of the building, down to the reclining chairs, light fixtures and washbasins, to perfection.

A remarkable use of light, harmony with the natural surroundings, curving forms, an unusual treatment of wood and youthful optimism characterize all of Aalto's buildings, from the Villa Mairea, a private residence (1938) in Noormarkku, to Säynätsalo Town Hall (1952), Jyväskylä University (1952–57) and the town centre of Seinäjoki (1960–87).

▼ The Villa Mairea is an L-shaped house designed by Alvar Aalto. The main floor was designed for receiving guests and the upper floor for family life. The garden features a sauna and a swimming pool of irregular shape.

of Reima Pietilä (1923–1993) and Raili Pietilä (b. 1926), such as the *Dipoli* students' centre and the Tampere Library, known as the *Capercaillie*, Classical harmony gives way to caprice and surprise. Meanwhile, old building methods, such as wood construction, are gradually coming into their own again, although traditionalism all too often takes the form of Postmodern quotations. Finland is still the promised land of Modernism.

Design

Finnish design was a household word in the 1950s and '60s. At the Milan Triennale in 1951, the year of the great breakthrough, Finnish designers won six Grand Prix, seven gold medals, eight silver medals and four honourable mentions. At the next few events, Finns took one quarter of all the awards on offer. Suddenly the names of Gunnel Nyman (1909–1948), Kaj Franck (1911–1989), Tapio Wirkkala (1915–1985) and Timo Sarpaneva (b. 1926) were on everybody's lips.

The new design idiom became the symbol of a new beginning for Finland, as the country emerged from the trauma of war and the dreary years of reconstruction. There was strong demand for modern utility objects. Finns had maintained strong emotional ties with their rural heritage, to which they returned in seeking renewed simplicity. Bridging the gulf between the traditional and the modern, designers combined the best of both, turning their back for good on the ostentation of the years between the wars.

Finnish designers also embraced the originally Swedish idea of "more beautiful everyday ob-

jects", giving pride of place to natural materials and uncomplicated forms. Louis Sparre (1863–1964) and other Art Nouveau designers at the turn of the century had devised a new look for furniture and ceramics, seeking inspiration in the traditional form of the *Kalevala* country, particularly East Karelia. This tradition is carried on today by the popular jewellery firm *Kalevala-koru*.

An even more influential model for the new generation of the '50s was Alvar Aalto, the leading architect of the organic Functionalist movement, who also designed most of the interiors of his buildings, including furniture and light fixtures. The interior decoration company Artek, founded by Aalto in 1935, initially concentrated on marketing Aalto's own designs. Some of its international classics were birch chairs and tables with legs made of bent plywood and the beautifully shaped, wavy Savoy vase.

Marimekko, a garment and

▼ The "Chanterelle" vase by Tapio Wirkkala.

► Marimekko's spring 1999 fashions still remain faithful to the stripes that made the company famous, although designers have changed over the years. The photo shows a design by Ritva Falla.

fabric store founded by Armi Ratia (1912–79), revolutionized the traditional ideas of good taste and correct colours. A spate of young, boldly experimental designers, including Maija Isola (b. 1927) and Vuokko Eskolin-Nurmesniemi (b. 1930), produced colourful but clean-lined fabrics and clothes which sealed Marimekko's international success.

Finnish utility ware took on a whole new look. Even the most ordinary Finnish home filled up with new design articles: glasses, vases, textiles, pots and pans, scissors and other objects which elsewhere represented rarefied elitism. Especially the ergonomically designed, orange-handled Fiskars scissors have been a fixture in every Finnish home since the 1960s. They are said to be the world's most plagiarized product.

In the 1950s Finland was like one great building site, and modern design provided the perfect match for the architecture of the new buildings. The design revolution also reflected more general social changes: a streamlined vase or a curtain with bold colours and patterns served to express their owners' new, more liberal attitudes.

Industry, too, contributed to the change, shifting the focus from expensive, unique *objets d'art* to serially produced and moderately priced utility objects.

The young generation of the 1990s has taken up the challenge of this recent past, cultivating a more relaxed attitude to tradition along with the now familiar, polished modernist idiom, and experimenting with an increasing range of natural and recycled materials.

Paper art made a rather late ap-

▼ Three brooches with animal motifs by Kalevala-Koru.

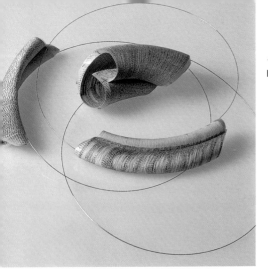

◀ Necklace made of a phone book, by Janna Syväoja.

pearance in Finland, but when it was taken up, the results were impressive. One of the leaders in the field is Janna Syväoja (b. 1960); like many other designers of her generation, she uses recycled paper to make elegant jewellery and other ornamental objects.

Art

Finnish art has been highly successful in merging national and international influences. The various isms have taken on a distinctly Finnish garb here, adapted to the local mentality, landscape and climate. Even the severest abstract modernism is imbued with the warmth of natural forms, as seen in the flowing lines of the sculptures of Kain Tapper (b. 1930) and others, reflecting the smooth surface of the Finnish bedrock.

The first Finnish painter to rise to European standard was Werner Holmberg (1830–1860), who studied in Dusseldorf in the 1850s. Before his time, the gentry commissioned their portraits from itinerant painters known as "counterfeiters," most of whom were of foreign origin. One of the best Finn-ish painters among them was Margareta Capsia (1682–1759), Finland's first woman artist. Mikael Toppelius (1734–1821) was a prolific religious painter who filled many churches in northern Finland with didactic religious imagery.

The Finnish artists of the late nineteenth century flocked to the studios of Paris, bringing back the fashions of outdoor painting and impressionism when they returned. The new continental style of painting, however, presented an almost insuperable challenge back in the home country: how to capture on canvas the cool, translucent northern light; the midnight sun in summer; the cold, glittering, blue lakes; the brooding forest, with spruce trees standing to attention in military fashion; the snow and ice with their endless shades of white? These were the problems tackled by painters such as Albert Edelfelt (1845–1905), highly successful in the salons of Paris and a precursor of impressionism in Finland, who also depicted the Finnish country people in images of idealized dignity.

The National Romantic and Symbolist movements of the turn

▶ The painting *The Wounded Angel* by Hugo Simberg in Tampere Cathedral.

▶ Akseli Gallen-Kallela's painting *Kullervo's Revenge.*

▲ *The Seamstress* by Helene Schjerfbeck.

of the century gave rise to the "golden age" of Finnish art. Akseli Gallen-Kallela (1865–1931) created an imagery from the *Kalevala* which is still part of the national identity. The drawings and watercolours of Hugo Simberg (1873–1917), Gallen-Kallela's pupil and protégé, are highly prized today. Simberg translated Finnish folk tales into a fairytale world of his own, peopled with little devils and wounded angels.

Women painters made their mark early in Finland. Fanny Churberg (1845–1892) was a bold stylist and colourist who paved the way for her younger colleagues, such as Maria Wiik (1853–1928) and Helene Schjerfbeck (1862–1945).

The Parisian-style naturalism introduced in Finland by Schjerfbeck and her "sister painters" aroused considerable controversy at the time. Over the years, Schjerfbeck developed into a highly individualistic, elegant modernist, whose work has only recently begun to gain the international attention it deserves.

The role of women in Finnish art has continued to grow. Today's pioneers, such as Marita Liulia (b. 1957) and Henrietta Lehtonen (b. 1965), work with new media, such as CD-ROM and video art.

Postwar Finnish art has been marked by a debate between Constructivism and Expressionism, intellectual control and emotional extravagance. The precise, carefully planned forms of Sam Vanni (1908–93), Juhana Blomstedt (b. 1937) and Matti Kujasalo (b. 1945) contrast with a pitiless dissection of emotions in the works of Aimo Kanerva (1909–91), Marika Mäkelä (b. 1947) and Marjatta Tapiola (b. 1951).

Today's young generation prefers to maintain an ironic distance from the archetypal Finnish images. A frequently seen guest at the international forums of the '90s is Esko Männikkö (b. 1959), a photographer specializing in portraits of humble northern folk – particularly lonely backwoodsmen – and a Vermeerean virtuoso of atmosphere.

Notable Finnish artworks can also be found outside galleries and museums. Although many of the wall paintings in the mediaeval greystone churches were hidden behind a coat of whitewash in the days of the Lutheran Reformation, some remarkably evocative frescoes from the early sixteenth century have been preserved, notably in the churches of Hattula, Lohja and Rymättylä. The colourful figures of saints in ancient altar screens were also destroyed after the Reformation, with the result that the interiors of most Finnish churches are extremely ascetic.

The country's oldest artworks, however, are rock paintings dating from between 3000 B.C. to the beginning of the Christian Era. They mostly depict game – elk, deer and bear – hunted and worshipped by the nomadic tribes of the north. The same motifs can be found in ritual objects, the finest of which are genuine works of art.

Music

Every now and then people ask how it is possible that a country the size of Finland can keep producing so many top-notch conductors, singers and musicians.

The answer is simple: Finland has a decentralized system of music institutes offering basic musical education around the country, even in small towns. The 150 institutes in the network, from north to south, sift out the country's musical talent most effectively.

The early history of Finnish music has little to boast about. There was no royal court, and therefore no court orchestra. Art music was generally confined to the manors and parsonages: the lowlier rural population sang, at home and in church, sometimes in

SIBELIUS

■ Jean Sibelius (1865–1957) was hailed in his day not only as a musical genius, but as the champion of a nation struggling for its independence.

He handled his PR job with aplomb. Seven symphonies, a violin concerto, *Finlandia* and *Valse triste* proclaimed the plight of the composer's native country around the world. *Kullervo*, *Karelia* and *Tapiola* were unabashedly patriotic works. Thus Sibelius's music came to be seen as representing northern emotions and nature.

Sibelius has always been well-loved in Finland and the Anglo-Saxon world. In recent years his music has also been gaining ground in France and Germany. Osmo Vänskä and the Lahti Symphony Orchestra have been showered with international awards for their renderings of the Sibelius Violin Concerto, *The Tempest*, *En saga* and the recently rediscovered tone poem *Skogsrået* (The Wood Nymph).

One of the leading performers of the Sibelius Violin Concerto is Pekka Kuusisto. In 1995, at the age of 19, he became the first Finn to win the International Sibelius Violin Competition, a prestigious event held only once every five years.

▲ *Portrait of Jean Sibelius* by Akseli Gallen-Kallela.

▲ Esa-Pekka Salonen.

WORLD STARS

■ There are surprisingly many Finns among the top conductors on the international circuit. Esa-Pekka Salonen (b. 1958) is chief conductor of the Los Angeles Philharmonic and Jukka-Pekka Saraste (b. 1956) of the Toronto Symphony Orchestra. Sakari Oramo (b. 1965) took over the Birmingham Symphony from Simon Rattle. While remaining faithful to the Lahti Symphony Orchestra, Osmo Vänskä (b. 1953) now also heads the BBC Scottish Symphony Orchestra in Glasgow. The youngest virtuoso is Mikko Franck (b. 1980).

There is something of a Finnish mafia in the opera world. The German opera houses alone have some forty Finnish singers on their payroll. Matti Salminen (b. 1945), Jorma Hynninen (b. 1941), Karita Mattila (b. 1960) and Monica Groop (b. 1958) are stars who appear regularly in the major opera houses of the world.

Pianists Ralf Gothóni (b. 1946) and Olli Mustonen (b. 1967) and cellists Arto Noras (b. 1942) and Jan-Erik Gustafsson (b. 1970) are among the numerous Finnish musicians who have forged an international career for themselves. Finland's leading orchestras include the Radio Symphony Orchestra (Helsinki), the Tapiola Sinfonietta, the Lahti Symphony Orchestra and the Central Ostrobothnian Chamber Orchestra (Kokkola).

▶ Karita Mattila in concert in the great snow castle in Kemi.

▲ Jukka-Pekka Saraste.

▲ Osmo Vänskä.

four-part harmony if the church had no organ.

The music of Bernhard Henrik Crusell (1775–1838), the "Northern Mozart", is still frequently played, but it was only with the emergence of Jean Sibelius (1865–1957) that Finnish music became more widely known.

The towering figure of Sibelius overshadowed his many talented contemporaries. The modernist opera *Juha* (1922) by Aarre Merikanto (1893-1958) was rediscovered only after decades of oblivion. Recently the works of Leevi Madetoja (1887-1947) and Erkki Melartin (1876-1937) have also enjoyed something of a revival.

Present-day Finnish composers go their own ways. Einojuhani Rautavaara (b. 1928), Kaija Saariaho (b. 1952) and Magnus Lindberg (b. 1958) are among those who have gained world fame. A special success story is that of contemporary Finnish opera. Among the most recent premieres was *Kullervo*, an opera by Aulis Sallinen (b. 1935) on a theme from the *Kalevala*.

A racy, outspoken quality is

▲ Apocalyptica. Infernal-symphonic heavy metal salvos on the cello.

SUMMER IS FESTIVAL TIME

■ IThe traditional, sleepy lakeside cottage holiday gave way in the 1960s and '70s to the bustle of summer music festivals, with opera in Savonlinna, folk music in Kaustinen, chamber music in Kuhmo, Naantali and Mustasaari, new music in Viitasaari, organ music in Lahti, rock in Ruissalo and jazz in Pori.

The combined attendance for all Finnish summer festivals is well over a million. Audiences are mostly Finnish, but the number of foreign visitors is growing, as the Savonlinna Opera Festival and the Kuhmo Chamber Music Festival, in particular, are widely considered to rank among the outstanding events in the world in their categories.

the hallmark of contemporary Finnish folk music. The female folk groups Värttinä and Me naiset have been particularly successful with this style.

Two of the leading young jazz bands are Trio Töykeät and Perko-Pyysalo Poppoo. Apocalyptica, a group of young musicians from the Sibelius Academy, plays heavy rock, but also resorts on occasion to a more melodious vein. A postmodern mix of languages is the hallmark of the Leningrad Cowboys, which occasionally performs together with the Red Army Choir from the former Soviet Union.

Dance

In 1921 Finland's cultural scene was abuzz: the founding of a national ballet as an extension of the Finnish Opera made the newly independent republic fully autonomous also in artistic terms.

The ballet's opening performance was *Swan Lake* – no surprise, considering that the whole project was the brainchild of Edvard Fazer (1861–1943), a former impresario of the Russian Ballet. Russia had already provided neighbourly encouragement before: the visits of St Petersburg's Mariinsky Theatre, in particular, had been hugely successful.

Meanwhile, new winds in the dance world were blowing from the West. Isadora Duncan enthralled her audience at the Finnish National Theatre in 1905. Inspired by Duncan's performance, Maggie Gripenberg (1881–1976) founded a free dance group which eventually gained international fame with her Sibelius choreographies.

The general public cared little

TANGO

■ As soon as the wartime ban on dancing was lifted, open-air summer dancing began to spread like wildfire in Finland. Platforms were set up in the green countryside, where waltzes and foxtrots resounded. The undisputed favourite, however, was the tango, which captured the emotional essence of the Finns, ranging from silent longing to blazing passion.

Tango buffs have had their own festival in Seinäjoki since 1985, with concerts, dances and contests regularly drawing over a hundred thousand aficionados.

The Finnish tango king Eino Grön (b. 1939) now has a crown prince in Jari Sillanpää (b. 1965), while thousands of aspiring hopefuls practice in the hundreds of karaoke bars that have sprung up around the country.

"Ladies' choice" is among the liveliest phenomena in Finnish popular culture. The purpose of the exercise is strictly confined to dancing. The ladies are of an independent ilk, so a gentleman who finds himself at such an event should not be alarmed if asked by a most respectable matron for the honour of a tango.

▼ The Finns adore the tango. The Tango Festival in Seinäjoki.

for the aestheticism of art dance. Only a handful of enthusiasts attended the performances of the much-vaunted modernists of the 1950s. The young radicals of the '60s, however, finally discovered the roots of the nation in dance. The free dance group Raatikko translated the classics of socially committed literature all the way back to Aleksis Kivi's seminal *Seven Brothers* (1980) into the language of dance. They also recycled the Icelandic writer Halldór Laxness's novel *Salka Valka*.

Ever since then, Finnish dance groups have sought to break with tradition or to reinterpret it, now turning the national epic, the *Kalevala*, into a comedy of manners, now projecting the *Kanteletar*, a collection of lyrical folk poetry, as a pageant of masculine bluster and feminine melancholy.

The high-water mark of Finnish dance came in the 1980s. The psychological dance dramas of Jorma Uotinen (b. 1950), such as *Forgotten Horizon* (1980) and *The Shout* (1985), initially met with bewilderment, then gradually with growing appreciation. Uotinen, who had been a member of Carolyn Carlson's group at the Paris Opera, was appointed head of the Helsinki City Theatre dance group in 1980. From there he was eventually snapped up to direct the National Ballet, bringing fresh ideas as the ballet moved to the superb new opera house in Helsinki.

A new, urban energy suffuses the work of Kenneth Kvarnström (b. 1963) and his dance group, while Ari Tenhula (b. 1964) makes use of the idiom of Japanese Buto, Arja Raatikainen (b. 1958) of shamanism and Tero Saarinen (b. 1964) of the theatre of the absurd and silent film. Sanna Kekäläinen (b. 1962) and Kirsi Monni (b. 1963) explore the perspective of modern women.

The Finnish dance scene converges in June on the town of Kuopio, in the midst of the Finnish lakeland. The Kuopio Dance and Music Festival provides a classy but informal annual overview of the state of the art.

The Kaustinen Folk Music Festival in July attracts over one hundred thousand tradition buffs yearly. New folk dance is no mere dainty tripping; it has an earthy, often downright boisterous quality about it.

Theatre

A veritable theatre fever possessed the Finns in the nineteenth century: every local club and association, even in the smallest of communities, had its own theatre performances and poetry recitals, or at least arranged visits to theatres in the towns. The first playhouses were built in Viipuri, Turku and Helsinki around the year 1800; soon amateur groups were appearing everywhere. Curiously enough, it seems that the stage is a place where the Finns, usually so introverted, can truly give vent to their feelings.

Nowadays there are some forty professional theatres in the country, the northernmost being in Rovaniemi, north of the Arctic Circle. Public subsidies have kept the theatre accessible to the whole nation; indeed, in this country of five million people almost three million theatre tickets are sold every year.

On average, about half the performances are of works by Finnish playwrights. The perennial favourites include the plays of Aleksis Kivi, Minna Canth (1844–1897), Maria Jotuni (1880–1943) and the Estonian-born Hella Wuolijoki (1886–1954), usually set among well-to-do farmers or the educated gentry.

New winds began to blow in the 1960s, particularly in the productions of independent theatre groups. Directors like Kalle Holmberg (b. 1939), Ralf Långbacka (b. 1932), Jouko Turkka (b. 1942) and Arto af Hällström (b. 1952) also went on to challenge the established tenets of institutional theatre. The big theatres are not afraid to take risks nowadays, although from time to time they must of course resort to popular hits to stay afloat.

The contemporary style emphasizes visual and physical elements. A certain distance from the dramatic heritage is cultivated in updated versions of the classics. Recent examples include a silent version of one of Minna Canth's well-loved Finnish rural dramas; performances by an all-female cast of Aeschylus, Shakespeare and Gogol; and stylized analyses of Dostoevskyan guilt or Tolstoyan ethics. A boldly experimental approach has infused these performances with new forcefulness and vitality.

Finland has a major international theatre forum in the Tampere Theatre. A summer event first held in 1968, it took on a new lease of life in the late eighties when Vivica Bandler, the *grande dame* of the Finnish theatre world and a tireless innovator, took over as artistic director.

▼ In his street theatre performance at the opening of the Tampere Theatre Festival, Reijo Kela wound up on a treetop.

Film

It is not easy to be a filmmaker in a country the size of Finland. Without government support, it would be virtually impossible, for very few films indeed can attract one hundred thousand viewers – the number required to turn a profit – in a country with a population of five million. And obviously Finnish films must rely on Finnish audiences.

Nonetheless, the Finnish film industry has survived, though on a modest scale. Ten films or so are now made in an average year, as against fifteen in the heady '80s.

The big commercial hits tend to be farces such as the *Uuno Turhapuro* films by Spede Pasanen (b. 1930). The Finns also love film versions of their literary classics, especially the war novels *Tuntematon sotilas* (The Unknown Soldier) by Väinö Linna (1920–1992) and *Talvisota* (The Winter War) by Antti Tuuri (b. 1944). The director Markku Pölönen (b. 1957) has won the Finns' hearts with his explorations of the Finnish mentality and the country's recent history, especially in *Kuningasjätkä* (Summer by the River). Renny Harlin (b. 1959) has made a career in Hollywood with films of action, horror and adventure, but has not had much success in his home country.

Among the currently active directors, the Kaurismäki brothers Aki (b. 1957) and Mika (b. 1955) have been particularly successful in Europe. Especially the cinephiles of France, Germany and Britain take pleasure in the

▲ The film *Valkoinen peura* (The White Reindeer) by Erik Blomberg from 1952 is the story of a Lapp witch. The main themes are the mystique of Lapland, all-consuming love and jealousy.

THE KAURISMÄKI BROTHERS

■ The opening in 1982 of Mika Kaurismäki's first feature film, *Arvottomat* (The Worthless), marked a milestone in the history of Finnish cinema: the slow, deliberately artificial speech, the stilted phrases, understated gestures and expressions and general use of clichés represented a new approach to filmmaking in Finland.

Later the director has tried his hand at more traditional films. Although *Rosso* (1985) is another story of an aimless wanderer, *Amazon* (1990), filmed in South America, takes a clear stand in favour of the rainforest and the global environment.

Aki Kaurismäki started his career in cinema as scriptwriter and assistant director for his older brother. In his own feature films, he has developed an even more pronounced stylization, with a strong sense of tradition and a curiously oblique humour. *Varjoja paratiisissa* (Shadows in Paradise, 1986), *Tulitikkutehtaan tyttö* (The Match Factory Girl, 1990) and *Kauas pilvet karkaavat* (Drifting Clouds, 1996), the latter something of an international hit, have already attained the status of modern classics.

▶ *Kauas pilvet karkaavat* (Drifting Clouds) is an elegiac film by Aki Kaurismäki which gives full expression to Kaurismäki's poetic, primitivistic style. In the final scene, the hero and heroine, previously unemployed, have just opened a restaurant of their own: the future, hope, clouds and faith blend in an ode to true love.

▲ Rauni Mollberg directed a pacifist adaptation of Väinö Linna's classic novel *The Unknown Soldier.*

extreme stylization, quiet irony and tragicomic humanist outlook of the Kaurismäkis' films.

The characters they love to depict are anti-heroes: lost, lonely, silent tramps who prefer the role of the perpetual loser to that of the glib yuppy. Despite the critical praise showered on them, the Kaurismäkis' films rarely reach a large audience; they are cult movies cherished by small groups of connoisseurs.

Auli Mantila (b. 1964) follows in the Kaurismäkis' footsteps, but has perhaps an even more uncompromisingly detached, spare style. Her first full-length feature film, *Neitoperho* (The Collector) has already won international recognition. It takes the form of a horror film, presenting a cheerless vision of modern man's spiritual homelessness and longing for love, building up to a powerful ethical statement.

Despite these notable contributions, the true golden age of Finnish film was back in the 1930s, a period that saw a whole spate of directors and actors who have taken on an aura of legend. Before his early death in the Winter War, Nyrki Tapiovaara (1911–1940) made cool, stylized film versions of the classics of Finnish literature, to which the bold, melodramatic effects of Teuvo Tulio (b. 1912) stood in complete contrast. Valentin Vaala (1909–1976) directed no less than 44 films; his register ranged from comedy to thriller and from folk drama to literary classic.

One of the most notable Finnish filmmakers of the latter half of the 20th century is Rauni Mollberg (b. 1929). His *Maa on syntinen laulu* (The Earth Is a Sinful Song) won international acclaim. Set in the remote backwoods of Lapland, this primitive love story conjured up a fierce vision of nature, sex, religion and guilt. Mollberg also directed a remake of Linna's great war novel, *The Unknown Soldier*. This was a daring enterprise considering that the earlier film, directed by Edvin Laine (1905–89), had come to be regarded as the definitive screen version. Mollberg succeeded in his intention of stirring up controversy, for his pacifist interpretation presented the Finnish soldier, not as a quick-witted hero, but as a sensitive, vulnerable youth, little more than a child. Buffeted by war and at the mercy of the vast, subarctic forest, the helplessness of the human condition takes on mythic proportions.

▲ The original Finnish edition of the novel *Sinuhe the Egyptian* by Mika Waltari.

Literature

Inspired by the National Romantic movement in the nineteenth century, the Finns raised literature to a pedestal even higher than that of art: it showed the nation the path to be followed, symbolizing the country's independent existence. It held up a mirror to show who we were and where we came from. Since the reflection was not always flattering, bitter literary wars broke out from time to time.

For many centuries, since the time of Finland's first writer known by name, the monk Jöns Budde (c. 1437–c. 1491), most of Finland's literature was written in either Swedish or Latin. It took a long time before a vernacular literature was created, although Finnish as a written language had existed since the Reformation, when Mikael Agricola (c. 1510–1557) published an ABC and translated the New Testament and other works into Finnish in the 1540s.

▼ Illustration by Erkki Tanttu to Aleksis Kivi's novel *The Seven Brothers*.

Only in the nineteenth century did Finnish literature really come into its own. J.L. Runeberg (1804–1877), who wrote in Swedish, created a poetic, idealized image of the Finnish peasantry as a pious and brave folk. Aleksis Kivi (1834–1872), who wrote in Finnish, saw his people in a more realistic and humorous light. His novel *Seitsemän veljestä* (The Seven Brothers) is still far and away the most popular classic of Finnish literature.

The electronic media represent a powerful rival to literature these

KALEVALA, THE FINNISH NATIONAL EPIC

■ Elias Lönnrot (1802–1884) published two seminal compilations of folk poetry, the epic *Kalevala* (1835) and the lyric *Kanteletar* (1840), both received with great excitement throughout the country – although the first readers could not make much of the difficult language, the educated classes being mainly Swedish-speaking.

The poems of the *Kalevala* are in trochaic tetrameter, a poetic measure believed to have originated some two thousand years ago. There is no rhyme, but regular refrains and alliteration serve as props for the memory. The language is lively and the characters are portrayed with care. Educators have been prompt to point out that the most important battles in the epic are waged with words rather than swords.

In fact the *Kalevala* is a distinctly feminine epic. The principal theme is human relations: love and sex, wooing and marriage. The women are strong, the men often weak and pathetic. And yet the epic also contrived to offer the Finns the heroes they craved. Especially the wise old Väinämöinen represents a model for spiritual values that was easy to appeal to in bringing the rustic Finns into the sphere of European civilization.

Far more folk poetry has survived than could be fitted into the two early collections. When the entire corpus was compiled and published between 1908 and 1948 as *Suomen kansan vanhat runot* (The ancient poetry of the Finnish people), the material filled 33 volumes.

The *Kalevala* has provided an inspiration for later folklore studies, too. In recent years, ethnographers have recorded modern culture, children's traditions, workplace traditions, war memories, urban stories and customs. The Finnish Literature Society's folk poetry archives – the world's largest of their kind – comprise some three million recorded poems. In the early 1990s, someone counted that the manuscripts alone filled 474 metres of bookshelves, in addition to which the archives have recordings and videos.

Especially during the nineteenth century, the *Kalevala* aroused an enormous enthusiasm for national culture among Finland's artists, designers, architects, composers and writers. They made long journeys on foot to the eastern parts of the country and as far as the villages of Russian Karelia. With the millennium approaching fast, folk poetry is now coming into its own again. The heroes of the *Kalevala* march across the stage in Finnish drama and opera. CD-ROMs, strip cartoons and world music based on *Kalevala* themes are cropping up apace in Finland and elsewhere, too. The Helsinki heavy

days. Nonetheless, the Finns are still among the world's most voracious readers. In an average year, more books are published per capita in Finland than in any other country. Most Finnish writers today use the Finnish language, but some write in Swedish and a handful in Sámi.

Things are not easy for Finnish writers: there are only five million speakers of Finnish, and Finnish books face a prohibitively high language barrier. All the same, an ever-increasing number of books manage to cross that

▶ Finnish artists have been inspired by the *Kalevala* for over a century now. Particularly impressive were the illustrations by Akseli Gallen-Kallela. In 1990, Hannu Väisänen discovered in the folk epic a heady mix of violence and aesthetics. The photo shows Väisänen's work *The Gold Cloth of the Maid of Pohja*: "Busy weaving cloth of gold, / Carefully the silver threading, / Weaving with a golden shuttle, / And a weaver's reed of silver."

metal band *Amorphis* is making a name for itself with rock music based on folk poetry. An album called *Tales from the Thousand Lakes*, likewise based on the *Kalevala*, has sold some one hundred thousand copies in Germany and the United States.

Indeed, it is our ethnic music that has probably gained most new friends. New folk song and instrumental ensembles keep appearing, some of the best-known being *Tallari*, *Värttinä*, *Me naiset* and *Loituma*. Even the venerable national instrument,

the *kantele*, has been dusted off and been given a new lease of life.

The annual review for this music is the Kaustinen Folk Music Festival, which started out in the 1960s as a showcase for the local fiddlers, but is now a megafestival of world music, attracting thousands of performers and one hundred thousand visitors to this small Ostrobothnian town every summer.

ADVENTURE IN MOOMIN VALLEY

■ Adventure and homecoming, friendship and solitude, the braving of danger and the warmth of the family hearth are the classic ingredients of Tove Jansson's storybook world. The combination of genuine fairy-tale and insightful character portrayal have made Jansson's books perennial favourites of children and adults alike.

Tove Jansson was born 1914 in Helsinki, the daughter of an artistic family. She studied painting, and invented the Moomintroll figure in the 1940s. The first Moomin book, *Kometjakten*, (Comet in Moominland) was published in 1945 with the writer's own illustrations. Jansson went on to publish a dozen other Moomin books as well as several novels and short stories for grown-up readers.

Nowadays the Moomin books are available in several dozen languages, and the Moomins have even ventured as far afield as Japanese animated films for television.

▲ Tove Jansson at the time she created the Moomins. In her hand is Moominmamma with her handbag, with several Moominpapas and Moomintrolls and the Snorkmaiden on the table.

THE FINN'S FAVOURITE HAUNT: THE LIBRARY

■ In the 1990s the Finns have broken virtually all the world records connected to public libraries. Finland has the highest number of registered borrowers, approximately one half of the population. The number of loans in proportion to the population is likewise high, some twenty books a year. The number of library visits – some six million a year – is also proportionally the world's highest.

The Finnish library network is exceptionally efficient and covers the whole country. Bookmobiles carry books even to the smallest villages hidden away in the vast forests. All the same, small municipal libraries, in particular, were hard hit by the recession of the early 1990s, although during it the number of users increased by ten per cent, and more in places. Although the number of foreign-language videos and works of poetry has had to be cut, lending is still free of charge.

▶ Mobile libraries serve readers in fringe areas. The Helsinki City Library received an award in 1998 for "The Most Beautiful Bookmobile".

barrier. The all-time international hit is the historical novel *Sinuhe egyptiläinen* (Sinuhe the Egyptian) by Mika Waltari (1908–1979), translated into 32 languages, which has cropped up on bestseller lists in various countries.

Friends of early 20th century poetry are familiar with the name of Edith Södergran (1892–1923), a Finn who wrote poetry in Swedish. This shy, consumptive but fiercely individualistic young woman arrived at a revolutionary free verse form independently at about the same time as Ezra Pound and T.S. Eliot in English.

Among the modernist poets of the 1950s, the outstanding figures were Paavo Haavikko (b. 1931), Eeva-Liisa Manner (1921–1995), Bo Carpelan (b. 1926), Veijo Meri (b. 1928) and Pentti Saarikoski (1937–1983). More recently, a racy northern exoticism, coupled with a longing for freedom, has found expression in the prose of Arto Paasilinna (b. 1942) and Rosa Lik-

▲ Pentti Saarikoski, an outstanding poet and translator – and the *enfant terrible* of his day.

som (b. 1958). The *Moomin* books of Tove Jansson (b. 1914) are international classics of children's literature.

The Midsummer writers' congress in Lahti has provided a biennial forum for East-West dialogue since the late 1960s.

Finland in the
21st century

In the latter half of 1999 it was Finland's turn to hold the rotating precidency of the European Union. To Finns, this had a powerful symbolic meaning. Exactly 100 years had passed since the Russian emperor issued his edict restricting Finnish self-rule, an act that at the time was believed to spell the end of Finland as a nation, but in fact was the beginning of the Finnish national struggle for an independent existence that has been carried on by a variety of means and at different levels of intensity ever since. Membership in the EU has finally provided Finland with a secure place among the independent states of Europe.

The conclusion may seem paradoxical: surely membership in the EU restricts Finnish sovereignty. But the sovereignty of small states like Finland has always been circumscribed by the realities of power. Membership in the EU grants them an influence, or at least a right to be heard they have not had before.

It would be wrong, however, to imagine that Finns go about their daily business feeling proud of the great gains their country has made during the twentieth century. My claim that Finland has emerged as a winner from the ordeals of the past 100 years may well be dismissed by many of my compatriots as hollow. They may argue that it is not such a great achievement to win a medal in a race in which most of the competitors have fallen by the wayside because of injuries or been disqualified for cheating. Rather than looking back, they are peering anxiously ahead, wondering what may be in store for them in the twenty-first century.

Not so long ago the answer would have been presented in the form of scenarios that would consist of three pillars: the first painting a picture of the future too good to be true and the second too horrible to contemplate, so we would settle for the third, which predicted partly cloudy weather with occasional showers and variable winds. But no scenario predicted the fall of the Berlin Wall, and since 1989 political scenarios have been out of fashion. Instead, forecasters have borrowed from modern physics the uncertainty principle: because random change is possible, the future is simply unpredictable. The only certainty is that change will continue.

With Europe in a state of flux, the future of Finland will depend on its ability to adjust to changing conditions. In this respect Finland has a number of important assets. It is a homogeneous, well-functioning, orderly society, with a civil service that overall is competent and efficient. Corruption is incidental, not endemic. The gap between income groups is narrower than in most other EU countries, which makes Finland an egalitarian society with a high degree of cohesion. As much as 14 percent of the government budget is spent on public education: this too contributes to social equality. The political system is stable. As the record shows, the Finns are a pragmatic people, not prone to fanaticism. Traditional civic virtues are still respected, and the Protestant work ethic prevails, though crumbling at the edges.

Industry and business are adjusting to changing conditions. Mergers are producing units large enough to compete successfully in the global markets. In the forest industry, for example, the former field of a dozen or more companies has been reduced to three giants, one of which (UPM-Kymmene) is now the biggest producer of paper and board in Europe and the second biggest in the world.

This points to a dilemma faced by small nations in this age of integration. Is a corporation big enough to be successful in the global market too big for Finland? UPM-Kymmene accounts for as much as 13% of Finland's total earnings of foreign currencies. There is an obvious danger in such a heavy dependence on one private company.

The challenge to national independence posed by the globalization of business will remain a sensitive issue. In Sweden, this was illustrated by the uproar caused by a statement from L. M. Ericsson, manufacturer of telecommunications equipment. Its CEO warned the Swedish government that the company might have to move its headquarters to another country because heavy taxation makes it impossible to recruit foreign staff to work in Sweden. He pointed out that Ericsson does not need Sweden, but Sweden needs the $7 billion of export income earned by the company.

The head of Ericsson's Finnish competitor, Nokia, took a different view, however. Mr. Jorma Ollila stated that Finland remained important to Nokia: "The people, the atmosphere, the education and the basic economic policies are right. Nokia's corporate culture, its underlying ethos and the strength of its product development are Finn-

ish." Although Finland accounts for only 6% of Nokia's total sales, more that 55% of its total workforce are in Finland, and 78% of its development staff are in this country. Since Nokia's share in Finland's total exports in 1997 is 15%, the national credo of Nokia's management has a profound political significance.

Nokia today is the world's leading mobile phone supplier and a leading supplier of mobile and fixed telecom networks, while Ericsson claims to be the world's largest supplier of telephone equipment. How is it possible that these two companies based in Nordic welfare states with high wages now share the commanding heights of the global mobile phone industry? *Time* magazine offered the answer in its July 14, 1997 issue. The Nordic countries, according to *Time*, got a head start in 1981 by launching the world's pioneering international cellular phone network, the Nordic Mobile Telephone system (NMT). But this is a superficial explanation. Why were they able to get a head start? The answer is in qualities of life mentioned by the Nokia chief. This proves that high-wage, social-welfare European countries can maintain their competitive edge on a high technological level. According to a OECD study, unit labour costs in high-tech industries in Finland have actually declined because very strong productivity growth has compensated for nominal wage increases. This partly explains why unemployment remains high while the economy is growing at a rate of 4% a year. It also points to the solution of this problem: education – a slow process.

The tax issue remains of crucial importance. High marginal tax, rising above 60 percent, hits the minority of Finns who by virtue of education and language skills are able to take advantage of the opportunities offered by the Common Market. Finland cannot afford a debilitating brain drain. But the demand for tax relief for the higher income bracket clashes with the egalitarian ideology behind the progressive tax systems in the Nordic countries. The government is determined to balance its budget by the year 2000 and then to begin to reduce public debt. Substantial tax reductions can only be achieved through cuts in spending. This, too, will be a slow process.

Adapting to change means becoming more like other countries. Every turn of the integrationist screw reduces distinctions. How far will this go? In an article devoted to the fiftieth anniversary of the Marshall Plan, OECD secretary-general Donald Johnston quoted the words of Canadian poet Frank Scott: "The world is my country, the human race my race." Johnston added: "When that becomes a conviction of all mankind, the Marshall vision will have been fulfilled." A terrifying vision – mankind homogenized.

So once again the Finns are told the end is near. This time it is not rape by Russian imperialism that is expected to put an end to the independence of Finland: the new enemy is globalization. In this view, the global technostructure of finance and industry will finally render the nation-state obsolete. The best and the brightest will drift to the great financial centres, perhaps keeping a summer cottage on a lake somewhere in Finland, while those left behind will lack the intellectual resources needed to maintain a distinct cultural identity. They will cease to be a nation; they will become a group of producers and consumers living in one corner of the Common Market.

The threat to national identity posed by economic integration is perceived in countries much bigger and more powerful than Finland. It has been graphically described by a French politician of the Left, Jean-Pierre Chevènement, who wrote in 1980 that if things went on as they were, by the year 2000 France would be a kind of Algeria appended to the United States, with the majority of the French, in berets, their litre of red wine and their Camembert in their pouches, continuing to speak French in mountain villages. One more scenario that has failed to materialize.

Obviously, economic integration creates an ever greater interdependence between states, and this inevitably reduces the scope of independent action. Every nation chafes from time to time under the constraints imposed upon it, while the advantages gained through economic integration are taken for granted. Yet the independence of Finland, measured by the capacity of its government to safeguard and promote the interests of its citizens, is surely now far greater than it was at the time when the country was poor, backward, and wholly dependent upon the export of forest products. As a small country, Finland has little say in the general trends of the world economy, but within the frames set by those trends, success or failure depends on its own performance – its ability to maximize the benefits of integration and minimize its negative effects. National independence has become a function of economic competitiveness.

This view is rejected by the Greens and other seekers of alternative lifestyles who believe the industrial world is heading toward a general breakdown. Why should Finland compete so strenuously for first-class passage on a ship that is bound to sink soon? They advocate the reduction of Finland's dependence on the world economy through a return to a simpler way of life that would save the natural environment from further destruction. Such a retreat from the evil world into the security of an inner citadel has been the dream of stoics and ascetics, religious leaders and revolutionary philosophers throughout the ages. It sounds vaguely appealing to those who long for some respite from the strains of competitive living, but its adherents remain a fringe group in Finland and elsewhere in Europe.

True, the global industrial technostructure not only obliterates the animal and vegetable diversity of our planet but endangers its human diversity as well. The number of languages in the world is shrinking: of the roughly 6500 languages now spoken, up to half are already endangered or on the brink of exstinction. Linguists estimate that a language dies somewhere every two weeks. According to one expert, the world stands to lose 95% of all its languages in the coming century.

The death of a language is fatal to national identity. The British writer and historian Jan Morris has written a heart-rending obituary on the loss of the Welsh language – "a treasure of Europe, with its own wonderful structure of literature, tradition, myth and legend, but also a lively, flexible, everyday working tongue". The pressures of integration, Morris wrote, threatening the national identity of Wales had been intensified beyond resistance.

Had Finland remained part of Sweden, Finnish might never have developed into a language of culture. But under Russian rule the Finnish language flourished, and attempts at Russification were successfully resisted. As an imperial power, Russia failed to exercise the kind of cultural influence that Britain and France had among their subject peoples. This is also shown by the survival of the Estonian language after 50 years of repression by the Soviets. There is no general rule: some languages and nations succumb to the pressures of integration and unification; others do not.

The Finnish language is now safely ensconced as one of the 11 official languages of the European Union. To permit representatives of each member state to use their own language is a cumbersome way of doing business: 33 interpreters are needed to translate 110 language combinations at a single meeting. In practice English, French and German are used as working languages. But to strike the language of a member state from the list of official languages would be an affront to the independence of that state: language makes a nation.

Has Finland now reached a point in history when the absence of external threats will begin to undermine its internal cohesion and weaken the sense of national purpose? There are as yet no obvious symptoms of this widespread post-Cold War infection. As newcomers to the European Union, the Finns feel they have to prove themselves as a serious partner. They retain a competitive attitude to international relations. And there is always the Big Neighbour. Unlike some other small nations living in safer and more comfortable environments, the Finnish people will not lack the stimulus of external challenges. This will keep the Finnish national spirit alive.

Index

Photographs

Cinemateca de Finlandia: pp. 151 (above), 152;

European Commisssion: 7, 9, 24;

Finnish Broadcasting Co. Archives/Ari-Pekka
Keränen: 146;

Finnish Film Archive:pp. 151 (above), 152;

Finnish Maritime Administration: p. 99;

Fotoni/Mikko Oksanen: pp. 125, 127, 129;

Hackman Designor Ltd.: p. 140:

Ulla Hassinen: p. 142;

Jari Jetsonen: p. 42;

Kalevala Koru Ltd.: p. 141 (thtee photographs);

Kemi Snow Castle: p. 33;

Kone Ltd.: 81;

Lehtikuva: pp. 10, 40, 55, 103, 134, 156 (below);

Lehtikuva/Jaakko Avikainen: 59;

Lehtikuva/Chad Ehlers: p. 109;

Lehtikuva/ Sari Gustafsson: pp. 21, 69, 113, 116,
117, 120;

Lehtikuva/Olli Herranen: p. 104 (below);

Lehtikuva/ Björn-Ove Holmberg: p. 39,

Lehtikuva/Martti Kainulainen: pp. 26, 44, 60, 71, 75,
76, 106;

Lehtikuva/Soile Kallio: pp. 15, 101, 132, 133, 148;

Lehtikuva/Juha Kärkkäinen: p. 22;

Lehtikuva/ Matti Kolho: pp. 30–31, 34 (above), 35,
38, 43 (above), 45, 115, 122, 123,126, 135, 158;

Lehtikuva/ Pentti Koskinen: pp. 87, 114;

Lehtikuva/Patrik Lindström: p. 112;

Lehtikuva/Kimmo Mäntylä: pp. 62, 67, 68, 89, 102,
104 (above), 111, 136, 137;

Lehtikuva/Matti Matikainen: p. 27;

Lehtikuva/Seppo Nykänen: pp. 77, 130;

Lehtikuva/Hans Paul: pp. 12 (above), 124;

Lehtikuva/Päivi Peltonen: p. 118;

Lehtikuva/Jorma Puusa: p. 139;

Lehtikuva/ Kimmo Räisänen: pp. 41, 88;

Lehtikuva/Ilkka Ranta: pp. 12 (below), 16;

Lehtikuva/Jukka Ritola: p. 107;

Lehtikuva/Pekka Sakki: p. 20;

Lehtikuva/Heikki Saukkomaa: pp. 56, 70–71, 119;

Lehtikuva/ Kai Tirkkonen: p. 90;

Lehtikuva/ Jarmo Tolonen: p. 43 (below);

Lehtikuva/ Hannu Vallas: p. 29;

Lehtikuva/Tor Wennström: p. 12 (centro);

Lehtikuva/Christian Westerback: p. 146 (two in the
middle);